LIVING COLOR
FOR YOUR GARDEN

The bright orange-red color of trumpet vine (Campsis radicans) *advertises a deep well of nectar in the tubular flowers, tailor-made for the long bill of a male Ruby-throated Hummingbird.*

Active, beautiful, and easy to observe, hummingbirds and butterflies are delightful additions to any garden. The motion of their wings brings a welcome sense of life, and their brilliant colors are as vivid as the flowers. As they visit your garden, you will find it fascinating to observe their daily habits, the unfolding of their life cycles, and their interactions with plants.

Fast-flying hummingbirds capture insects in midair as do their closest relatives, the swifts, but they also obtain a large share of nourishment from flowers—in the form of nectar and insects. As enjoyable in the garden as hummingbirds, butterflies also are drawn to flowers for nectar. And they seek out plants on which to lay their eggs.

Butterflies and hummingbirds are more than mere ornaments to flowers—both in the garden and in the wild. When hummingbirds dip deep into a blossom, they often become dusted with pollen, which is then transferred to the female part of a flower, pollinating the bloom so that it can produce seed.

Colorful hummingbirds and butterflies may visit a garden at the same time, but they are different from one another in their life cycles as well as the types of plants they seek and the habitats they need to raise the next generation. That's why this book is divided into two main sections: one on attracting and understanding hummingbirds, and the other about butterflies.

The Monarch and other butterflies seek clusters of flowers to find the most nectar in a small area. *This swamp milkweed (Asclepias incarnata) also serves as food for Monarch caterpillars.*

Each section begins with a description of the interesting physical characteristics and the unusual lives of these fabulous creatures in the wild—their anatomy and their coloration, their food preferences and habitat needs, their life cycles, and their intriguing behavior. The second part of each section provides instructions for incorporating the needs of hummingbirds or butterflies into an inviting garden.

Because plants and habitat are vital, each section offers many suggestions for preferred plants—in lists, design plans, and plant galleries. You also will find detailed advice for adding supplemental food sources, such as special sugar-water feeders for hummingbirds and overripe fruit for some butterflies, as well as water, shelter, and perching and basking places, to make your yard even more appealing. The hummingbird and butterfly galleries pinpoint details for attracting each species to the garden.

Although the needs of hummingbirds and butterflies are different, it is easy to create a garden that attracts both, no matter how big or small your landscape. The rewards will arrive soon: perhaps a Broad-tailed Hummingbird visiting your hanging basket or a Black Swallowtail taking nectar from a butterfly bush.

Hummingbirds and butterflies in your garden will provide you with hours of pleasure as well as an invaluable connection to the natural world. The first step to inviting them is to learn about the habits and needs of these fascinating creatures.

Plentiful nectar flowers and sunny, open space attract butterflies to this meadow of sunflowers, phlox, asters, and coneflowers.

THE NATURE OF HUMMINGBIRDS

Found only in the Americas, hummingbirds are remarkable birds with intriguing habits. The species that will grace your garden vary depending on where you live. This chapter presents the story of hummingbirds in the wild: their history and range, their brilliant plumage and other remarkable physical features, and why their flight and feeding methods are perfectly adapted to the difficult feat of obtaining nectar from flowers. You'll get a peek into their private lives as the chapter describes courtship and nesting. And the "Gallery of Hummingbirds" on pages 14 to 17 provides a close-up look at the needs of nine North American species.

It's a win-win relationship: The bird gets nectar, the plant gets pollinated. Hummingbird flowers, such as the Cape honeysuckle (Tecomaria capensis), *above, have protruding stamens (male organs) tipped with pollen-covered anthers. As the Anna's Hummingbird, above, probes for nectar, its head is dusted with so much pollen it looks like a yellow cap. When the bird visits the next blossom, pollen adheres to the stigma (female organ), pollinating the plant. Concentrated abundance, such as the hardy fuchsias, at right, will keep hummingbirds lingering.*

Frequent refueling is a must for high-octane hummers. A king-size feeder accommodates a crowd of Calliope Hummingbirds and a single male Broad-tailed Hummingbird.

NAMES AND CLASSIFICATION

Prior to the discovery of the New World, hummingbirds were unknown in Europe. So it is no wonder the early Spanish explorers gave them such imaginative names as *aves varias*, "many-colored birds," and *joyas voladores*, "flying jewels." New England colonists—inspired by the buzz the birds make with their wings—were the first to call them hummingbirds.

During the 18th century, when Carolus Linnaeus, a Swedish naturalist, devised a system of scientific names, hummingbirds were placed in a family of their own, the *Trochilidae*. The name comes from a Greek word, *trochilos*, or small bird.

Hummingbirds that are closely similar to one another are placed in the same genus. For example, the Ruby-throated Hummingbird of the East and its western counterpart, the Black-chinned Hummingbird, both belong to the genus *Archilochus*. The species name serves to separate one kind of hummingbird within a genus from another. Colorful Latin names such as *Amazilia beryllina* (the Berylline Hummingbird) are matched by equally colorful common names: Lucifer, Magnificent, Calliope, and Volcano Hummingbirds, and the Magenta-throated Woodstar, Rufous-crested Coquette, Green-breasted Mountain-gem, and Golden-crowned Emerald. The names are in keeping with the awe that these gemlike birds have always inspired.

DISTRIBUTION

Hummingbirds are native to the Americas. They originated in northwestern South America, then spread north into Central and North America and south into Brazil. Today there are approximately 340 species. Ecuador has 163, the largest number in any country.

Of the 21 species that reach the United States, 16 breed here, another is a regular visitor, and 4 others are regarded as strays—only occasionally present. The largest number of species is found in the mountainous regions of western Texas, New Mexico, and Arizona. Of those that breed in North America, only 10 species have ranges that extend a significant distance north of the Mexican border (see the "Gallery of Hummingbirds," beginning on page 14). Only a single species, the Buff-bellied Hummingbird, breeds in south Texas. The Ruby-throated is the only hummingbird that is known to breed east of the Mississippi. Except during migration, hummingbirds are not likely to be found in the Great Plains region of the United States and Canada.

Four species reach Canada, and one, the Rufous Hummingbird, breeds as far north as Alaska. The greatest traveler of all is the Ruby-throated Hummingbird, whose range extends as far west as Alberta, east to Nova Scotia, and south through the eastern United States. To reach wintering grounds in Mexico and Central America, the Ruby-throated Hummingbird flies across the Gulf of Mexico, returning to nest by the same route.

HUMMINGBIRDS ON THE MOVE

As human population—and gardening—have expanded, so have the ranges of some hummingbirds. In parts of the West, where wildflowers disappear with the coming of the dry season, ornamental landscape plants have become immensely important. The popularity of sugar-water feeders is also having an effect.

Two species have expanded their ranges dramatically in recent years. Anna's Hummingbird, once restricted to southern California, the slopes of the Sierra Nevada, and the San Francisco Bay Area, has moved southward, eastward, and northward within the last 50 years. The birds now breed in coastal Oregon and Washington, southwestern British Columbia, and Arizona.

The Rufous Hummingbird has shown a change in wintering range, which is normally in western Mexico. Once a rarity along the Gulf Coast and in the Southeast, the Rufous Hummingbird now appears by the hundreds in those areas every year. Researchers believe that the population of this species in the Southeast will continue to climb, so if you live in the area, be sure to watch for these beautiful rust-and-orange hummingbirds.

PLUMAGE

Brilliant gorgets beautify and help identify male hummingbirds. Clockwise from top left: Anna's Hummingbird flashes neon pink; Costa's, violet; Magnificent, green; and the well-named Blue-throated Hummingbird vivid blue.

Charles Darwin was so struck by the dazzling plumage of the hummingbirds he saw in South America that he compared them to the renowned birds of paradise. He attributed their bright colors to sexual selection, females choosing more brightly colored males over less colorful ones. This explanation is only partially correct; hummingbirds are colorful regardless of gender. And in some species (mostly those of the Tropics) the male and female look exactly or almost exactly alike.

IRIDESCENCE

In keeping with their small size, hummingbirds have small feathers. They are closely packed but not interlocked by feather tips (barbules), as in most other birds.

In most birds plumage color is integral, created by pigments in the feathers. Much of the brilliant color for which hummingbirds are famous, however, is from iridescence, which is more the result of feather structure than feather pigment.

The iridescent colors of their feathers have earned hummingbirds such names as "flying jewels." Iridescence is caused by the reflection of light upon minute air-and-melanin-filled feather structures called platelets. Depending

COLOR IS CAMOUFLAGE

It is not an accident of nature that most daytime nectar feeders, including hummingbirds and butterflies, are brightly colored. Their colors match those of the bright flowers they visit. Although a vivid patch of pink or orange feathers might stand out like neon against a dull background, it makes excellent camouflage in a group of bright blooms. Combine camouflage colors with small size, and hummingbirds are definitely difficult for predators to spot among flowers. At the nest, the green back of most female hummingbirds blends with the foliage in the sight of any predator peering down through the branches. Protective coloration, as well as swift flight, makes hummingbirds poor targets for birds of prey.

The male Rufous Hummingbird, at right, is surprisingly difficult to see from a distance as it collects nectar from a flowering spike of red hot poker.

on how the light strikes the platelets and the angle at which they are viewed, different color effects are produced.

Nearly all of the hummingbird's feathers are iridescent, but some parts of the plumage are much more brilliantly colored than others.

MALE AND FEMALE PLUMAGE

In male hummingbirds, the most vivid plumage is found in the gorget, a brightly colored feathered area on the throat. The Ruby-throated, Blue-throated, Black-chinned, and Berylline (from the sea green color of the mineral beryl) Hummingbirds are all named for the distinctive color of their gorgets.

Like other hummingbird feathers, the gorget gets its brilliant hue from iridescence, so it is dependent on light to ignite the feathers into blazing color. Depending on how the light strikes it, the gorget may appear intensively colored or almost black. A gorget that glows a ruby red most of the time can change to an iridescent blue, a metallic green, and a reddish-purple before turning back to the original bright red. The colors change as the bird is viewed from different angles and in different light. On a cloudy day or when the bird is in the shade, the gorget, like the other plumage, appears dark and without color.

In addition to colorful gorgets, males of many tropical species sport prominent crests, long tail streamers, and other adornments that capture the attention of the female during courtship.

Female hummingbirds lack the brilliant gorget of the male, yet compared to the females of many other bird species, they are often brightly colored, with feathers that flash with iridescence in the light. Females must not be overly visible to predators as they sit on their nests and go about their domestic duties. At the same time, like the male, they should blend in well with the flowers they visit. The compromise most often seen in female North American species is iridescent green above and grayish white or white below. Females in most hummingbird species have white corners at the tips of their outer tail feathers.

Adult male hummingbirds, with their bright colors, gorgets, and other markings, can be identified with comparative ease if seen under good light conditions. But North American female hummingbirds are difficult to identify as to species. They have only a few plumage characteristics that are helpful in distinguishing one species from another. Size, voice, length and shape of bill, and, in some species, color of bill are useful clues.

PLUMAGE IN YOUNG

During their first few days in the nest, young hummingbirds are featherless except for two downy rows on the back. The air movement from their mother's wings moves these feathers and alerts the young that their mother is near; they then beg for food. By the time the young birds are ready to leave the nest, they are well-feathered and resemble the adult except for a lack of iridescence. Before the first molt, which takes place at the end of the breeding season, young males have a mixed plumage, showing some characteristics of each parent. The young female, on the other hand, has a similar dress both before and after the molt. She looks exactly like her maternal parent.

The plumage of a pair of young Broad-tailed Hummingbirds is similar to their mother's, a trait typical of the young of nearly all species. Iridescence and, in males, bright colors are acquired as the birds mature.

ANATOMY

Like other hummingbirds, this male Ruby-throated can extend its long tongue and roll it into a tube to collect tasty tree sap or nectar. Bony internal structures move the tongue in and out like a spring.

Many of the hummingbird's remarkable achievements are due to its unusual anatomy. Its wing structure is unlike that of other birds and enables it to hover and to fly both forward and backward. The bill and tongue also distinguish the hummingbird from other birds. Perfectly adapted to the hummingbird's feeding habits, they are indispensable in gaining nectar from deep, tubular flowers. Blossoms of this shape that open in the daytime are primarily adapted for pollination by hummingbirds. Thanks to the hummingbird's special adaptations, these flowers can be pollinated swiftly and well, and the hummingbird is rewarded with nectar.

HUMMINGBIRD TONGUE AND HYOID APPARATUS

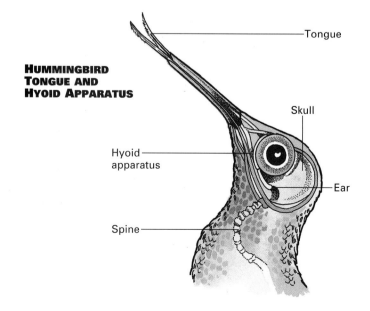

Tongue

Skull

Hyoid apparatus

Ear

Spine

A hummingbird's bill is long, tubular, slender, and usually straight or curved downward (decurved). Besides using their bills as tools for probing flowers and catching insects, hummingbirds use them as weapons. They are pugnacious birds and are quick to threaten opponents with their bills.

The bill varies in length, shape, and coloration from species to species. Hummingbirds that nest in North America have average-length bills that range from about ½ inch to 1 inch in length. The Andean Swordbill, a South American species, holds the record, with a bill that measures up to 4 inches in length.

Bills of species that nest in North America are either straight or slightly decurved. The bill of the Lucifer Hummingbird, which nests in the Chisos Mountains of western Texas, is the most decurved. In one species the bill is curved upward.

As its name suggests, the Broad-billed Hummingbird has a wider bill than that of other North American species. The Broad-billed is more of an insect eater than other species, and its bill is thought to be an adaptation for capturing insects on the wing.

Hummingbird bills are either black or red or a combination of the two colors. The Buff-bellied, Violet-crowned, White-eared, and Broad-billed Hummingbirds sport red bills with black tips; the others have black bills.

THE TONGUE

Butterflies often spend a leisurely five seconds or more at blossoms rich in nectar, but hummingbirds zip in and out in a fraction of this time. The bird's specialized tongue allows it to drain the nectar quickly. If a blossom is unrewarding, a hummingbird recognizes this instantly and moves on to another.

As a hummingbird hovers, it thrusts its bill into the floral opening. The tongue does the rest. As specialized as any part of the hummingbird's anatomy, the tongue is deeply split at its tip. This tip is folded into a tube when the bird feeds. Nectar is not sucked up but held in the tubular portion and swallowed when the tongue is returned to the mouth. After it has emptied the nectary of the flower, the hummingbird flies off to make the rounds of more blossoms.

Like woodpeckers, hummingbirds have a bony structure called the hyoid apparatus attached to the tongue. This pair of bony coils serves to extend the tongue for considerable lengths and pull it back in again.

Tiny insects in flowers are withdrawn by the tongue with the help of saliva and, in some hummingbird species, by the fringe of tiny bristles found at the edges of the tip of the tongue.

VOCALIZATION

Hummingbird songs are uttered so rapidly that the human ear perceives them as high-pitched squeaks, chirps, and twitters—although some tropical hummingbirds do have songs that are considered appealing by human standards. Songs are learned, and there are identifiable regional differences among them.

Hummingbirds also produce distinctive wing noises due to air rushing through the feathers during flight. These wing sounds are helpful in identifying different hummingbirds, especially if the bird is hidden from view. For example, the male Broad-tailed Hummingbird produces a musical buzzing sound with its wings as well as a cricketlike trill. The beating of the wings of the female Broad-tailed produces a humming sound. The male Rufous Hummingbird produces a high trilling buzz with its wings.

WINGS AND FLIGHT

Hummingbirds have achieved a mastery of the air that combines the flight skills of both birds and insects. Their long, narrow wings, shaped for fast flight, are propelled by muscles that make up 25 to 30 percent of their body weight. Other birds can generate power only on the downstroke, but hummingbirds—because of the way their wings are attached with a rotating joint at the shoulder—can move freely in any direction: forward, backward, or hovering in midair.

The aerial courtship displays of male hummingbirds, in which the bird makes U-shaped nose dives at high speed, are astonishing feats of flight. Hummingbirds also perform aerial displays to frighten away intruders from a nesting territory or food site. To the intruder, the tiny hummingbird may seem like an attacking wasp or hornet.

The normal flight speed of hummingbirds—between 25 and 30 miles per hour—is not extraordinary, but the speed at which their wings beat is faster than any other bird. As many as 80 beats per second have been recorded in forward flight and 200 beats in display dives, when some species of hummingbirds may reach a speed of 65 miles an hour. The wings move so fast that they

appear as a blur when the birds are flying or hovering in front of a flower.

Hummingbirds make long, nonstop flights during migration; the Ruby-throated Hummingbird, for example, flies across the Gulf of Mexico each year to its wintering grounds in Mexico and Central America. Although many birds fly as far and farther, journeys of this length were once thought to be impossible for birds this small. Powerful wing muscles and fat reserves for fuel are the secrets behind this ability.

Caught in midstroke, a male Anna's shows the specialized anatomy of its wings. A single wing joint at the shoulder gives great flexibility, so that the bird can hover or instantly change directions.

Although they may seem like perpetual-motion machines, hummingbirds do sit still at times. The feather in its beak indicates that this Blue-throated Hummingbird has been preening. Before legal protection was enacted, hummingbird feathers were used in jewelry.

LIFE CYCLE AND FOOD REQUIREMENTS

Through a variety of survival adaptations, including torpidity (see page 13), hummingbirds have evolved to be quite long-lived. In the wild they have been known to live up to 5 years. Ages of 9, 10, and 15 years have been recorded in captivity.

Hummingbirds go through the same stages of courtship, mating, and nesting that other birds do. They are among the earliest nesters of American birds. The Anna's Hummingbird of the West begins courtship rituals as early as December. The Costa's and Allen's Hummingbirds, with ranges in southern parts of the Southwest and California, respectively, begin nesting as early as mid-February. On the Palos Verdes peninsula of California, both species breed the year around.

As big as its mother, a Broad-tailed Hummingbird fledgling still begs for food. The female bird builds the nest, incubates the eggs, and rears the young. The male's only role is to contribute his genes during mating.

DANGERS FOR HUMMINGBIRDS

Hummingbirds have few enemies. Their small size and quick flight make them poor targets for birds of prey, although a cat lying in wait can cause their demise. There are reports of hummingbirds nabbed by dragonflies and mantises and caught in spiderwebs. Cowbirds, which disrupt the nesting of other birds, do not lay their eggs in hummingbird nests as they are too small. Jays and snakes usually overlook the well-camouflaged nest.

A bigger hazard for hummingbirds is window glass: Like other birds, they notice only the reflection of the surroundings and fail to see the glass, resulting in often-fatal window strikes.

Hummingbirds also face danger from the weather. Cold temperatures, prolonged rainy spells, dry weather that causes flowers to wither, and storms during migration can cause a drop in the population.

The impact of the changing landscape and the use of herbicides and chemical sprays is hard to assess but could also be adverse. Chemicals kill small insects that the birds feed upon and may be ingested by the birds through nectar or from residues on flowers.

COURTSHIP

The hummingbird nesting season gets under way with elaborate "sky dances" of loops, swoops, and dives performed by the male. These spectacular display flights, which differ from species to species, are used to impress the female and to ward off males and other birds. One of the most spectacular displays is that of the Calliope Hummingbird, the smallest of all North American hummingbirds, which rises to a height of 60 to 90 feet, suddenly dives toward the ground, and, transcribing a wide arc, rises once again to the same height. The bird makes a loud whistle at the bottom of each impressive dive.

In most species the male performs his aerial dances throughout the nesting season and sometimes longer. Females sometimes conduct similar performances. Although the male hummingbird is highly attentive to the female during courtship, after having inseminated her he moves on, often to mate with another female. He takes no part in nest-building or in the rearing of young birds. The female is highly territorial and drives other hummingbirds, including the sire of the brood, from the nesting area.

THE NEST

The tiny nest, usually only 1½ inches in outer diameter, is cup-shaped, lined with plant down, and held together with spiderweb. The outside of the nest is camouflaged with bits of moss and lichen, so that it is virtually indistinguishable from the branch to which it is attached. It takes the female about a week to build. Many species anchor their nest to the top of a horizontal tree limb, where it looks like a natural protrusion. Some nest in vines, on large fern fronds, and even on light fixtures.

Masterfully camouflaged with bits of lichen bound with spiderweb, this Ruby-throated Hummingbird nest is at maximum occupancy with two nestlings.

THE BENEFITS OF SPIDERS

A healthy garden attracts a myriad of insects, which in turn attract spiders who come to feed on them. That's good news for hummingbirds, which seek out spiderwebs for two reasons: food and nesting material. Both the spider itself and the insects in its web are eaten by hummingbirds, which hover before the web to snatch a snack. During nesting season, most hummingbirds seek out spiderwebs to use as nest-building material. The birds begin nest-building by laying a foundation mat of sticky web to hold the nest in place on the limb or other support. Spiderweb strands are also used to bind the bits of lichen and other nest materials together, making a tough, compact cup.

Most place their nest where overhead shelter offers some protection.

In some species, notably the Rufous and Calliope Hummingbirds, the female often builds her nest on top of the one she built the year before. As many as four such nests, representing four consecutive years of nesting, have been recorded.

EGGS AND YOUNG

The two, sometimes three, elongated, pure white eggs are about ½ inch in length—large in comparison with the small size of the parents. Eggs are incubated for approximately 15 to 17 days. The newborn birds are blind and nearly featherless, and remain in the nest for about three weeks. Toward departure time the nest often becomes too small to hold the growing youngsters and they perch on the rim.

One brood is typical in most species, but the Allen's and Rufous have two broods per season and the Anna's and Black-chinned as many as three. Species that have more than one brood begin nesting early in the year and have their last brood in late summer to early fall.

FEEDING

Their bodies operate at extremely high speeds, so hummingbirds need a lot of fuel. To maintain a high rate of metabolism (the highest of any warm-blooded animal except shrews), they must feed every 10 minutes or so during the day. One bird visits hundreds of flowers each day.

Hummingbird flowers evolved at the same time as hummingbirds, developing specific features that allow hummingbirds access and exclude pollinators of other kinds. The flowers of these plants are tubular, scentless, brightly colored (often red), and easy for hummingbirds to hover before. Some flowers are shaped to accommodate hummingbirds with specialized characteristics, such as very long or short bills.

Hummingbirds cannot survive on nectar or sugar-water solutions alone. Insects are an essential protein source. The birds' migrations coincide with the blooming seasons of favorite flowers and the presence of small insects. On the wing they capture spiders in webs, insects that live on flowers, and tiny flying insects.

Keep your feeder filled in fall. After most of their kind have migrated, juvenile birds, such as this Ruby-throated Hummingbird, may still arrive, seeking nectar.

HUMMINGBIRD TORPOR

Hummingbirds—along with swifts and nightjars, their two closest relatives—have the unusual ability to slow their bodily functions and go into a kind of trance or torpor. At night when the birds can no longer feed or during periods of stress, they slow their metabolism to conserve energy.

During periods of torpor the heartbeat slows from as many as 1,260 beats per minute to only 50 beats per minute. There are periods when a torpid bird does not breathe, is stiff and numb, and to all appearances, is dead. A hummingbird may remain in this condition overnight and for most of a day.

The ability to become torpid is of great survival value. Hummingbirds frequently become torpid at night, and when day comes they quickly revive. Hummingbirds found in a torpid condition during a cold day revive if provided with warmth. They remain active as long as they can find food.

GALLERY OF HUMMINGBIRDS

Male Ruby-throated Hummingbird at Indian paintbrush (Castilleja spp.)

The descriptions and photographs that follow discuss the eight most common hummingbird species that range well northward into the United States and Canada, plus one other species, the Blue-throated Hummingbird, which breeds in mountainous areas of the United States near the Mexican border.

Like all hummingbirds, the nine species described in this gallery are members of the same family. They are listed alphabetically by common name. Each description mentions the key habits and characteristics of the hummingbird that will help you provide the right conditions in your garden for attracting it. Included are details of its preferred habitat,

UNCOMMON VISITORS

Sightings of uncommon hummingbirds are a special surprise, especially if you live in the Southwest, far West, or South. Texas is a hot spot for uncommon birds because of its proximity to the usual ranges of Mexican species. Several hummingbirds have limited breeding ranges in the United States; others are considered rare visitors. Some of the common North American hummingbirds featured in this gallery have also been noted in areas far from their usual homes, such as the Rufous Hummingbird, a western bird that sometimes appears in the East. If you see a bird you aren't familiar with, make a quick note of identifying features, then check a field guide. Some of the more unusual hummingbirds that may grace your garden include these species:

Bahama Woodstar
Berylline Hummingbird
Black-crested Coquette
Broad-billed Hummingbird
Buff-bellied Hummingbird
Cuban Emerald
Green Violet-ear
Green-breasted Mango
Lucifer Hummingbird
Magnificent Hummingbird
Plain-capped Starthroat
Violet-crowned Hummingbird
White-eared Hummingbird
Xantus's Hummingbird

A GUIDE TO THE RANGE MAPS

The range of each hummingbird species featured in the gallery is shown on the accompanying range map for that species. The breeding range (spring and summer) is shown in gold. The winter range is shown in purple (most species winter in Mexico, Central America, and South America, although a few winter in southern areas of the United States). The permanent range (areas where a species may be seen all year) is shown in green.

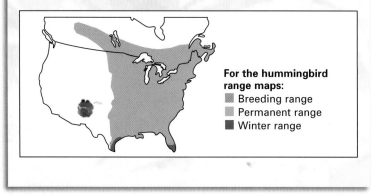

For the hummingbird
range maps:
■ Breeding range
■ Permanent range
■ Winter range

nesting and courtship behaviors, and favorite nectar plants.

Each description is accompanied by a photograph presenting a male in breeding plumage, and a map showing the areas in which the species is found. For more detailed identification information consult one of the many excellent field guides to birds (see page 33 for suggestions).

Remember that unusual weather or other occurrences may cause hummingbirds to stray outside their normal ranges. Especially in southern areas of the United States, keep your eyes open for rarities that may show up in your hummingbird-friendly yard.

The more familiar you become with the habits and preferences of the hummingbirds in your area, the more successful you will be in attracting them to your garden and in understanding their fascinating behavior.

SELASPHORUS SASIN

Allen's Hummingbird

Frequents moist coastal areas. Spring migrants follow the coast northward; fall birds follow mountain foothills southward. Nesting begins February.

NESTING: Monterey pines, live oaks, redwoods, and eucalyptus trees commonly chosen as nest sites. Normally nests away from human habitations, but there are records of nests on rafters, in vines on houses, and other such sites. Once the nest is built, the Allen's freely enters yards and gardens. Nest is made of fine rootlets, dry leaves, willow down, and hair held with spiderweb and camouflaged on the outside with lichens, at almost any height. It raises one or two broods a season.

FAVORED PLANTS: The Allen's Hummingbird visits a wide variety of wildflowers and garden plants, including California fuchsia (*Epilobium canum* ssp. *canum*), cape honeysuckle (*Tecomaria capensis*), century plant (*Agave americana*), western columbine (*Aquilegia formosa*), Indian paintbrush (*Castilleja coccinea*), madrone (*Arbutus menziesii*), scarlet monkey flower (*Mimulus cardinalis*), scarlet sage (*Salvia splendens*), and tree tobacco (*Nicotiana glauca*).

Allen's Hummingbird perching

CALYPTE ANNA

Anna's Hummingbird

This is a year-round resident in most areas and a common backyard bird. It may appear in coastal Texas and Louisiana.

NESTING: Females nest in yards, chaparral thickets, wooded canyons, and low, wooded slopes, often choosing groves of live oaks. Males tend to have separate territories in more open areas. Nest is made of plant down held with spiderweb, often lined with feathers and studded with lichens. It is placed on the upper side of a tree branch or in other locations, including outside lighting fixtures. The earliest North American hummingbird to nest; eggs may be laid in December. The courtship display, in which the male rises up to 120 feet and dives at a speed of up to 65 miles per hour, may occur any time of year. Raises two or three broods each season.

FAVORED PLANTS: Favorite flowers include coral bells (*Heuchera* spp.), eucalyptus (*Eucalyptus* spp.), fuchsia (*Fuchsia* spp.), flowering quince (*Chaenomeles* spp.), fuchsia-flowered gooseberry (*Ribes speciosum*), penstemon (*Penstemon* spp.), pineapple sage (*Salvia elegans*), tree tobacco (*Nicotiana glauca*), and woolly blue curls (*Trichostema lanatum*).

Anna's Hummingbird at Autumn sage (Salvia greggii)

ARCHILOCHUS ALEXANDRI

Black-chinned Hummingbird

Frequenting cities as well as wild areas, this bird may remain over winter on the Gulf Coast or in Southern California.

NESTING: Nests along watercourses or dry creek beds in sycamore, cottonwood, oak, willow, or alder in wild and semi-urban habitats, from hot, low-elevation cities to nearby mountain slopes. Also nests in ornamental trees and shrubs around human habitations. Nests have been recorded in odd locations, such as a hanging coil of rope or an outdoor lighting fixture. Nest is composed of soft plant material such as the yellowish down from the underside of sycamore leaves and the silky strands from milkweed seeds, held together with spiderweb. Raises two, even three broods each season. Courtship display consists of wide arcs, similar to the Ruby-throated Hummingbird.

FAVORED PLANTS: Canna (*Canna* spp.), century plant (*Agave americana*), chuparosa (*Justicia californica*), columbine (*Aquilegia* spp.), garden balsam (*Impatiens balsamina*), paloverde (*Cercidium* spp.), shrimp plant (*Justicia brandegeana*), tree tobacco (*Nicotiana glauca*), and yucca (*Yucca* spp.).

Black-chinned Hummingbird at bouvardia (Bouvardia glaberrima)

LAMPORNIS CLEMENCIAE

Blue-throated Hummingbird

Blue-throated Hummingbird at Texas sage (Salvia coccinea)

This species breeds in southwestern mountains. It may nest as late as October. Males are often found at higher elevations.

NESTING: Frequents wooded canyons, usually near streams. Nests in almost any place where overhead shelter is available: under rock ledges, eaves, bridges, and water towers, beneath tree branches, and inside buildings. Males often stay at somewhat higher elevations, where wildflowers are more plentiful. The nest is built out of plant fibers, cotton materials, mosses, and weed stems bound with spiderweb.

It is large for a North American hummingbird nest, up to 3 inches high and 2½ inches wide. As many as three broods are raised during a nesting season, which can last as late as October. During courtship, males fan their blackish tails, clearly showing the conspicuous white tips. They also deliver a squeaky song while perched.

FAVORED PLANTS: Flowers most commonly visited include century plant (*Agave* spp.), gilia (*Gilia* spp.), lobelia (*Lobelia* spp.), lupine (*Lupinus* spp.), penstemon (*Penstemon* spp.), scarlet sage (*Salvia splendens*), and tree tobacco (*Nicotiana glauca*).

SELASPHORUS PLATYCERCUS

Broad-tailed Hummingbird

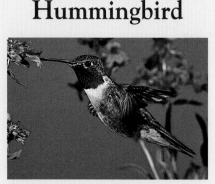

Broad-tailed Hummingbird at penstemon (Penstemon virens)

One of highest-altitude nesters—to 12,700 feet. Many move to high altitude after nesting. Migrates across Great Plains or along mountaintops.

NESTING: Resident of rugged mountain terrain with cliffs, canyons, and rushing streams. Adapts to whatever vegetational cover is present: pinon pine and juniper at lower elevations, pine and oak or aspen, Douglas fir, and ponderosa pine higher up. Nests near water and where wildflowers are abundant. Nest is made of plant fibers, moss, shreds of bark, and

down from the undersides of leaves. Peak nesting, beginning as late as May, coincides with blooming of favorite wildflowers; one or two broods are raised. During courtship, male rises 20 to 40 feet and makes a U-shaped, shallow dive or repeatedly circles his territory.

FAVORED PLANTS: Preferred flowers include blue larkspur (*Delphinium scopulorum*), century plant (*Agave* spp.) figwort (*Scrophularia* spp.), gilia (*Gilia* spp.), lousewort (*Pedicularis canadensis*), lupine (*Lupinus* spp.), nasturtium (*Tropaeolum majus*), sage (*Salvia* spp.), ocotillo (*Fouquieria splendens*), and penstemon (*Penstemon* spp.).

STELLULA CALLIOPE

Calliope Hummingbird

Male and female Calliope Hummingbirds

The smallest North American hummingbird. Nests at elevations as high as 11,500 feet. Follows spring bloom north up coast; fall migration coincides with mountain wildflower bloom.

NESTING: Nests at the edges of mountain streams and adjacent to glades and meadows, in pines, alders, spruces, and other conifers. During migration, appears in a wider range of habitats, including irrigated lands and gardens. Nest is made of bark, leaves, moss, and fine down from leaves and stems of plants. Nest resembles a pinecone

and is frequently placed on top of a cluster of cones, where it is nearly indistinguishable. Often built on top of previous year's nest. Nest is well-insulated to protect the female from cold at high elevations. During courtship display, male rises to considerable height and dives; may also make U-shaped flights or hover over intruders before giving chase.

FAVORED PLANTS: Visits a wide range of flowering plants, including columbine (*Aquilegia* spp.), currant (*Ribes* spp.), lousewort (*Pedicularis canadensis*), monkey flower (*Mimulus* spp.), orange (*Citrus sinensis*), penstemon (*Penstemon* spp.), and sage (*Salvia* spp.).

CALYPTE COSTAE

Costa's Hummingbird

Residing year-round in Southern California, this common species of southwestern deserts may move east to the Texas and Louisiana coasts in winter.

NESTING: Less dependent upon water than other North American hummingbirds and therefore better able to withstand desert conditions. Equally at home in urban districts, having adapted well to irrigation and settlement. In deserts, often nests in dead yuccas. Nest is made out of plant down and possibly feathers, pieces of paper, and dry leaves held together with spiderweb. In some coastal districts of Southern California, nesting gets under way in December; usual time is March or April. Male defends a large territory of 2 to 4 acres.

FAVORED PLANTS: Somewhat limited in its choice of flowers because its bill is too short to probe long floral tubes. Among the flowers that it visits are lemon bottlebrush (*Callistemon citrinus*), chuparosa (*Justicia californica*), coral bells (*Heuchera sanguinea*), Mexican bush sage (*Salvia leucantha*), ocotillo (*Fouquieria splendens*), scarlet larkspur (*Delphinium cardinale*), and tree tobacco (*Nicotiana glauca*).

Costa's Hummingbird

ARCHILOCHUS COLUBRIS

Ruby-throated Hummingbird

The only species that nests east of the Mississippi. It may winter in Florida and along the Gulf Coast. Occasional winter stragglers are recorded northward; keep feeders up through late fall.

NESTING: Nests in woodland openings, parks, and gardens. The nesting population often increases where feeders are in good supply.

Nest is built out of downy plant material, bud scales, and leaves, with lichens on the outside surface, anchored with spiderweb onto the top of a horizontal tree limb. One or two broods are raised in a season. During courtship, male rises 10 to 15 feet, then dives in a U-shaped arc, coming up again to about the same height. At the bottom of the dive, he makes a loud buzzing noise.

FAVORED PLANTS: Bee balm (*Monarda didyma*), Canadian columbine (*Aquilegia canadensis*), gladiola (*Gladiolus* spp.), nasturtium (*Tropaeolum majus*), red buckeye (*Aesculus pavia*), silk tree (*Albizia julibrissin*), trumpet creeper (*Campsis radicans*), jewelweed (*Impatiens capensis*), and trumpet honeysuckle (*Lonicera sempervirens*). In spring, before many flowers are in bloom, it feeds on sap flowing from holes made in trees by woodpeckers.

Ruby-throated Hummingbird at self heal (**Prunella vulgaris**)

SELASPHORUS RUFUS

Rufous Hummingbird

The most widely distributed and abundant western hummingbird. It may travel 3,000 miles on migration.

NESTING: Nests in woodland dominated by conifers with openings where wildflowers grow. Nest site may be close to human habitation. During migration it visits a wide variety of habitats, including orchards and gardens. It may stop for a week or more on migration where food is plentiful. Nest is made of moss, willow down, and rootlets held together with spiderweb and covered with lichens. During courtship, males make a series of oval-shaped dives with a loud buzz on the downswing, followed by a whining note and then a rattle. Males guard nesting as well as feeding territories.

FAVORED PLANTS: One of the most eagerly sought is red-flowering currant (*Ribes sanguineum*). Others include flowering maple (*Abutilon* spp.), bee balm (*Monarda didyma*), cape honeysuckle (*Tecomaria capensis*), columbine (*Aquilegia* spp.), fuchsia (*Fuchsia* spp.), larkspur (*Delphinium* spp.), lupine (*Lupinus* spp.), paintbrush (*Castilleja* spp.), and penstemon (*Penstemon* spp.).

Rufous Hummingbird at Indian paintbrush (**Castilleja** *spp.*)

HUMMINGBIRDS
IN THE GARDEN

High-voltage perennials—red hot poker, daylily, crocosmia, penstemon, and geum, plus cool-colored catmint and butterfly bush—signal a nectar feast year after year.

Offer a bountiful supply of nectar at feeders and flowers, and you are sure to attract hummingbirds. This chapter presents a host of enticing hummingbird flowers—from annuals, perennials, and wildflowers to vines, shrubs, and trees that provide shelter and nest sites as well as nectar. The plant gallery and additional lists at the end of this chapter make it easy to select the plants right for you and your garden.

Design ideas to entice hummingbirds to linger and perhaps nest in your yard are offered throughout this chapter, including ways to use water to attract the birds to bathe and drink, and instructions for setting up a small-scale program on a balcony or patio.

Sugar-water feeders are a sure-fire way to attract hummingbirds. This chapter shows you how to choose and use them, how to maintain them, and where to place them for maximum enjoyment.

Creating a garden that appeals to hummingbirds brings continuing pleasure. Once hummingbirds discover your tempting garden, they'll return year after year, often in ever greater numbers.

LONG-TERM COMMITMENT

Once you start inviting hummingbirds to your yard, they will come back day after day. When they return in spring after migration, they will look for flowers and feeders in the exact places they visited the year before. If your welcome mat is no longer out, they will waste precious energy seeking a new source of food. If you must be away during a critical time—especially early spring, when flowers are scarce, or nesting season— ask a friend to look after the garden and refill feeders so that your hummingbirds don't go hungry.

NECTAR FLOWERS

The sweet secretion called nectar is the reward that brings pollinators to flowers. Because pollinating animals come in all shapes and sizes, flowers use tricks such as fragrance and color to attract pollinators that suit their needs.

Nectar-rich hummingbird flowers need no fragrance to attract their feathered pollinators. They depend on the color red, or orange-red, orange, or pink, to attract hummingbirds. Hummingbirds have learned the red lesson so well that even red plastic attracts their attention. To a hummingbird, red means food.

Shape and form is another strategy that flowers use to target hummingbirds as pollinators. The tubular blossoms, often long and narrow, are structurally designed to be accessible only to the long bill and tongue of a hummingbird. The flowers are often positioned in open clusters that jut out or dangle from a plant so that hummingbirds can feed without hitting their wings against foliage. In some plants, the flowers are pendant, their openings accessible only to a bird or an insect that can hover below and turn its head upward to feed.

Butterfly flowers, although also tubular and rich in nectar, are usually fragrant and offer perches or platforms where the butterfly can settle when feeding. Purple, lavender, yellow, orange, or white and sometimes red are the colors that advertise good butterfly blossoms. Flowers that are blue, yellow, violet, or in the ultraviolet range attract nectar-seeking bees.

Many hummingbird flowers are ideal for the garden, and their bright colors are one of the best enticements you can offer to resident and migrant hummingbirds. A whole bed of scarlet sage, for example, can hardly escape notice. This doesn't mean that your garden must be all red. Once hummingbirds are accustomed to visiting, they will learn which flowers offer nectar and will visit them regardless of color.

Even the best hummingbird flowers do not always produce a good flow of nectar. If the weather is too hot or cold, too wet or dry, or the wind is very strong, the production of nectar slows or stops. To make sure that hummingbirds find plenty of nectar in your garden, plant a variety of flowers and an abundance of the best ones.

Flowers that face outward, free of impeding foliage, are perfectly positioned for a hovering hummingbird, as a male Broad-tailed Hummingbird demonstrates at scarlet gilia (Ipomopsis aggregata). Planting flowers with multiple blossoms results in longer hummingbird visits.

RED AND ORANGE FLOWERS FOR HUMMINGBIRDS

Hummingbirds must be able to recognize good nectar flowers immediately, and red is a reliable clue. Cape honeysuckle (*Tecomaria capensis*) shows its appeal to a Costa's Hummingbird, bottom right. Feeders use the same trick to attract patrons such as the Blue-throated Hummingbird, top right.

Aloe (*Aloe* spp.)
Bee balm (*Monarda didyma*)
Canadian columbine (*Aquilegia canadensis*)
Cape fuchsia (*Phygelius capensis*)
Cardinal flower (*Lobelia cardinalis*)
Coral bells (*Heuchera* spp.)
Coral tree (*Erythrina* spp.)
Fire pink (*Silene virginica*)
Flowering quince (*Chaenomeles* spp.)
Four-o-clock (*Mirabilis jalapa*)

Gilia (*Ipomopsis aggregata, I. rubra*)
Gladiola (*Gladiolus* spp.)
Impatiens (*Impatiens* spp.)
Jewelweed (*Impatiens capensis*)
Maltese cross (*Lychnis chalcedonica*)
Mexican sunflower (*Tithonia rotundifolia*)
Parrot's beak (*Lotus berthelottii*)
Pineapple guava (*Acca sellowiana*)
Red hot poker (*Kniphofia* spp.)

Scarlet bugler (*Penstemon centranthifolius*)
Scarlet larkspur (*Delphinium cardinale*)
Scarlet monkey flower (*Mimulus cardinalis*)
Scarlet sage (*Salvia splendens*)
Texas sage (*Salvia coccinea*)
Trumpet creeper (*Campsis radicans*)
Trumpet honeysuckle (*Lonicera sempervirens*)
Western columbine (*Aquilegia formosa*)

Feeders mimic the color, arrangement, and nectar reward of hummingbird flowers.

HUMMINGBIRD PLANTS

Flowering plants that provide many blossoms and a long season of bloom are the backbone of the hummingbird garden. Bloom in spring and late summer is vital for migrating hummingbirds. Along migration routes, red wildflowers are abundant at these times. Year-round bloom

Mexican pink (Silene laciniata), shown here, and similar California pink (S. californica) attract hummingbirds such as this male Calliope with its flashy streaked throat.

is important in mild-winter regions of the West where some species overwinter, and along the Gulf Coast, where the Ruby-throated Hummingbird and a number of western species are now spending the winter in increasing numbers.

Variety is key in establishing a garden attractive to hummingbirds. Try to offer many different flowers with hummingbird appeal over the longest season possible.

NECTAR FROM AROUND THE WORLD

Many native plants from North America (including Mexico) have evolved as hummingbird flowers. A number of plant families, especially the mints (*Labiatae*), buttercups (*Ranunculaceae*), and figworts (*Scrophulariaceae*), include many species that hummingbirds find irresistible. A variety of excellent native plants bloom late in the season, offering nectar to fall migrants.

Most native hummingbird plants fit well into any garden. Others, such as jewelweed (*Impatiens capensis*), are best in natural plantings, where they can spread freely. Some natives are difficult to establish in a garden and are best enjoyed as special wildflowers.

Plants that are native to other countries, known as "exotics," may also hold abundant supplies of nectar. Most hummingbirds are native to Central and South America, so many of the flowers from those lands are ideal. Although Africa, Australia, and Asia may not have the Americas' hummingbirds, they do have a good selection of nectar-rich flowers that the birds readily adopt. Exotics from subtropical areas (such as many popular garden annuals) are often long-blooming. The climates in their native lands are mild, and the plants have adapted to flower year-round.

No matter where it's from, a hummingbird plant is classified like other plants: as an annual if it blooms and dies in a single year; a perennial if it lives for two or more years; or as a vine, shrub, or tree.

LATE-BLOOMING NATIVES

Plant these natives for flowers from late summer through fall:
Autumn sage (*Salvia greggii*)
Bee balm (*Monarda didyma*)
Bouvardia (*Bouvardia* spp.)
California fuchsia (*Epilobium canum* ssp. *canum*)
Cardinal flower (*Lobelia cardinalis*)
Humboldt County fuchsia (*Epilobium septentrionale*)
Maryland figwort (*Scrophularia marilandica*)
Mexican bush sage (*Salvia leucantha*)
Penstemon (*Penstemon* spp.)
Pineapple sage (*Salvia elegans*)
Rose mallow (*Hibiscus moscheutos, H. grandiflora*)
Salvia confertiflora
Scarlet larkspur (*Delphinium cardinale*)
Scarlet monkey flower (*Mimulus cardinalis*)
Scarlet sage (*Salvia splendens*)
Texas sage (*Salvia coccinea*)
Trumpet creeper (*Campsis radicans*)

LONG-BLOOMING EXOTICS

Begonia (*Begonia* spp.)
Bottlebrushes (*Callistemon* spp.)
Cape honeysuckle (*Tecomaria capensis*)
Coral tree (*Erythrina* spp.)
Flowering maple (*Abutilon* spp.)
Flowering tobacco (*Nicotiana* spp.)
Fuchsia (*Fuchsia* spp.)
Hibiscus (*Hibiscus* spp.)
Impatiens (*Impatiens* spp.)
Lantana (*Lantana* spp.)
Powder-puff (*Calliandra* spp.)
Red hot poker (*Kniphofia* spp.)
Silk tree (*Albizia julibrissin*)
Weigela (*Weigela* spp.)

Try this island of annuals for a hummingbird magnet all summer long. Clockwise from top: spider flower, pineapple sage, white petunia, scarlet sage, parrot's beak, and apple-scented geranium.

ANNUALS

Annuals grow fast, usually flowering several weeks after sowing, and die after setting seed or with the onset of cold weather. Their long blooming season and showy flowers have made them extremely popular as border plants and in beds and window boxes. Many annuals are easy to grow from seed, or you can buy plants from garden centers.

Annuals can take more work in planting and preparing soil than other plants, but most gardeners feel that they are well worth the effort because they produce many flowers for a long time. Those on the list below will flower until frost in cold-winter areas. Scarlet runner bean and annual lupine have relatively short blooming seasons but are good hummingbird plants. Scarlet runner bean blooms from mid- to late summer; lupine has a peak blooming season in June. Interestingly, marigold, one of the most commonly planted annuals, has no hummingbird appeal, although it is attractive to some butterflies.

Many plants that gardeners in cold-winter regions think of as annuals, such as impatiens, begonias, and petunias, are actually tender perennials. In mild areas, these frost-sensitive plants live for years. Hummingbird-attracting plants of this type are also included on the list of annuals for hummingbirds at left.

This immature Ruby-throated is dining at annual Salvia coccinea (Texas sage).

ANNUALS FOR HUMMINGBIRDS

Annual larkspur (*Consolida* spp.)
Annual phlox (*Phlox drummondii*)
Begonia (*Begonia* spp.)
Flowering tobacco (*Nicotiana* spp.)
Garden balsam (*Impatiens balsamina*)
Geranium (*Pelargonium* spp.)
Impatiens (*Impatiens* spp.)
Mexican sunflower (*Tithonia rotundifolia*)
Nasturtium (*Tropaeolum majus*)
Petunia (*Petunia* spp.)
Pineapple sage (*Salvia elegans*)
Scarlet sage (*Salvia splendens*)
Spider flower (*Cleome* spp.)
Texas sage (*Salvia coccinea*)
'Victoria' salvia (*Salvia farinacea* 'Victoria')
Zinnia (*Zinnia* spp.)

HUMMINGBIRD PLANTS
continued

A Broad-tailed Hummingbird visits penstemon in a New Mexico meadow garden that pairs Indian paintbrush and penstemon.

PERENNIALS

Perennials are the backbone of most gardens. Unlike annuals, they live for years. Most perennials bloom for only a few weeks, however, so it takes some planning and experimentation to fill your garden with nectar-rich perennial flowers throughout the growing season. Use annuals or nectar feeders to fill in any gaps in bloom.

In cold areas, perennials die back in winter, then come up again in spring. Although many are easy to grow from seed, they are slower to start than annuals, so many gardeners depend on purchased plants. Consider color, height, and light and soil preferences as well as hardiness and disease resistance when you're choosing perennials.

Many of the best perennial hummingbird flowers are American natives, including columbine, coral bells, delphinium, cardinal flower, fire pink, and bee balm. A number of the western wildflowers favored by hummingbirds are perennials with long blooming seasons, including Indian paintbrush, penstemon, California fuchsia, monkey flower, and most of the sages.

Other common garden perennials also have strong appeal for hummingbirds. Daylily, hibiscus, gladiola, canna, red hot poker, phlox, hollyhock, fuchsia, and many others tempt hummingbirds to linger.

Sometimes sold as perennials, the plants known as biennials live only two years, producing a rosette of leaves the first year and flowering the second. One of the best biennials for hummingbirds is the native skyrocket, or scarlet gilia (*Ipomopsis rubra*). Living up to its common name, it shoots to a dazzling 6 feet, topped with bright scarlet trumpet flowers. This plant is difficult to transplant but easy to grow from seed. In dry, sandy soil, it will sow itself year after year.

This simple red, white, and blue dooryard garden of vines (trumpet honeysuckle) and perennials ('David' white garden phlox, 'Gartenmeister Bonstedt' red fuchsia, and blue catmint) can reward visitors with a hummingbird greeting.

PERENNIALS FOR HUMMINGBIRDS

Aloe (*Aloe* spp.)
Alum root (*Heuchera micrantha*)
Bee balm (*Monarda didyma*)
California fuchsia (*Epilobium canum*)
Cardinal flower (*Lobelia cardinalis*)
Century plant (*Agave americana*)
Columbine (*Aquilegia* spp.)
Coral bells (*Heuchera* spp.)
Culinary sage (*Salvia officinalis*)
Daylily (*Hemerocallis* spp.)
Delphinium (*Delphinium* spp.)
Figwort (*Scrophularia coccinea*)
Fire pink (*Silene virginica*)
Four-o-clock (*Mirabilis* spp.)
Fuchsia (*Fuchsia* spp.)
Gilia (*Ipomopsis aggregata, I. rubra*)
Gladiola (*Gladiolus* spp.)
Great blue lobelia (*Lobelia siphilitica*)
Hibiscus (*Hibiscus* spp.)
Hollyhock (*Alcea rosea*)
Indian paintbrush (*Castilleja* spp.)
Indian pink (*Spigelia marilandica*)
Maltese cross (*Lychnis chalcedonica*)
Monkey flower (*Mimulus* spp.)
Ocotillo (*Fouquieria splendens*)
Penstemon (*Penstemon* spp.)
Phlox (*Phlox* spp.)
Red hot poker (*Kniphofia* spp.)
Rose campion (*Lychnis coronaria*)
Sage; salvia (*Salvia* spp.)
Scarlet larkspur (*Delphinium cardinale*)

VINES

Vines are an excellent way to get a lot more flowers into your garden in a small amount of space. Cover a fence, arbor, trellis, or wall with flowering vines such as the vivid red cypress vine (*Ipomoea quamoclit*) and you will add hundreds more nectar-filled blossoms for hummingbirds. Most vines grow fast, especially annual species such as hyacinth bean (*Lablab purpureus*), which can cover a structure in a single season.

Like annual garden flowers, annual vines generally bloom until frost stops them in their tracks. Many perennial vines, such as the beautiful native trumpet honeysuckle (*Lonicera sempervirens*), also have a long blooming season. And even when they're not in flower, their foliage may support spiders and insects for hummingbirds to dine upon.

Vines make a garden look more interesting by adding height. They can separate feeding areas, so that a territorial hummingbird doesn't claim your entire yard. Trellised vines can serve as wind blocks, too, or provide shade for a pleasant sitting area.

Annual vines are easy to grow from seed sown directly in the garden. Perennial species are usually set in place as plants. Provide a structure that will support the vines you choose: Annuals will do well with even a light trellis, whereas perennials need a much sturdier structure. Annual vines are also ideal for planting in pots, a trick that may bring hummingbirds even to a second-story balcony. Mandevilla, a tropical perennial often grown as an annual pot plant in the North, is a superb hummingbird magnet for small spaces.

VINES FOR HUMMINGBIRDS

Canary creeper (*Tropaeolum peregrinum*)
Chilean glory flower (*Eccremocarpus scaber*)
Cross vine (*Bignonia capreolata*)
Cypress vine (*Ipomoea quamoclit*)
Hyacinth bean (*Lablab purpureus*)
Mandevilla (*Mandevilla splendens*)
Nasturtium (*Tropaeolum majus, T. peltophorum*)
Red morning glory (*Ipomoea coccinea*)
Red trumpet honeysuckle (*Lonicera × heckrottii*)
Scarlet runner bean (*Phaseolus coccineus*)
Scarlet trumpet honeysuckle (*Lonicera × brownii*, including 'Dropmore Scarlet')
Spanish flag (*Ipomoea lobata*)
Trumpet creeper (*Campsis* spp.)
Trumpet honeysuckle (*Lonicera sempervirens*)

This cottage-style mixed border will have hummingbirds waiting in line. In back are blue delphiniums, violet spider flowers, and pink hollyhocks. In midrange are columbines, four-o-clocks, and coral bells. Mounding nasturtiums edge the front.

Vigorous perennial trumpet creeper (Campsis radicans) is welcomed by hummingbirds.

HUMMINGBIRD PLANTS
continued

Nectar-generous shrubs add up to hummingbird heaven: orange Cape fuchsia (Phygelius capensis), red Salvia greggii, and purple butterfly bush (Buddleia spp.).

A southwestern hummingbird courtyard with diverse plants and open space. Clockwise from upper right: silk tree, pale pink flowering maple, rosemary, desert willow, fuchsia, coral tree, citrus.

TREES AND SHRUBS

Trees and shrubs provide not only shelter but also nesting sites and materials, such as plant fibers, soft down from undersides of leaves, and lichens. Some of the best nectar sources are the flowers of woody plants.

A number of species offer nectar at seasons when hummingbirds most need it—in winter and early spring, when other flowers may be scarce. The blossoms of orange trees nourish hummingbirds that overwinter in Florida, southern Texas, and Southern California. Winter jasmine (*Jasminum nudiflorum*), camellia, and the early blossoms of red-flowering currant (*Ribes sanguineum*), flowering quince, and some of the native azaleas (such as pinxterbloom azalea and flame azalea) also provide nectar.

In California, where the Allen's, Anna's, and Costa's Hummingbirds overwinter, eucalyptus trees are a popular source of food. Red-flowering gum (*Eucalyptus ficifolia*) blooms all year, and the swamp mahogany (*Eucalyptus robusta*) and several other species bloom in winter.

During late summer, when hummingbirds are preparing for the long flight southward, the blossoms of butterfly bush provide a welcome food source. Although butterfly bush is an outstanding butterfly plant, its flowers are also a favorite of hummingbirds and sphinx moths.

TREES AND SHRUBS FOR HUMMINGBIRDS

Arizona honeysuckle (*Lonicera arizonica*)
Beautybush (*Kolkwitzia amabilis*)
Bouvardia (*Bouvardia* spp.)
Butterfly bush (*Buddleia davidii*)
California fuchsia (*Epilobium canum* ssp. *canum*)
Camellia (*Camellia* spp.)
Cape fuchsia (*Phygelius capensis*)
Cape honeysuckle (*Tecomaria capensis*)
Carolina rhododendron (*Rhododendron minus*)
Citrus (*Citrus* spp.)
Coral tree (*Erythrina* spp.)
Desert willow (*Chilopsis linearis*)
Flame azalea (*Rhododendron calendulaceum*)
Flowering maple (*Abutilon* spp.)
Flowering quince (*Chaenomeles* spp.)
Fuchsia (*Fuchsia* spp.)
Hibiscus (*Hibiscus* spp.)
Orange bush monkey flower (*Mimulus aurantiacus*)
Pineapple guava (*Feijoa sellowiana*)
Pinxterbloom azalea (*Rhododendron periclymenoides*)
Powder-puff (*Calliandra* spp.)
Red buckeye (*Aesculus pavia*)
Red bush monkey flower (*Mimulus puniceus*)
Red-flowering currant (*Ribes sanguineum*)
Rose of Sharon (*Hibiscus syriacus*)
Rosebay rhododendron (*Rhododendron maximum*)
Salmon bush monkey flower (*Mimulus longiflorus*)
Twinberry (*Lonicera involucrata*)
Weigela (*Weigela* spp.)
Western azalea (*Rhododendron occidentale*)
Winter jasmine (*Jasminum nudiflorum*)
Yellow honeysuckle (*Lonicera flava*)

THE HUMMINGBIRD-FRIENDLY YARD

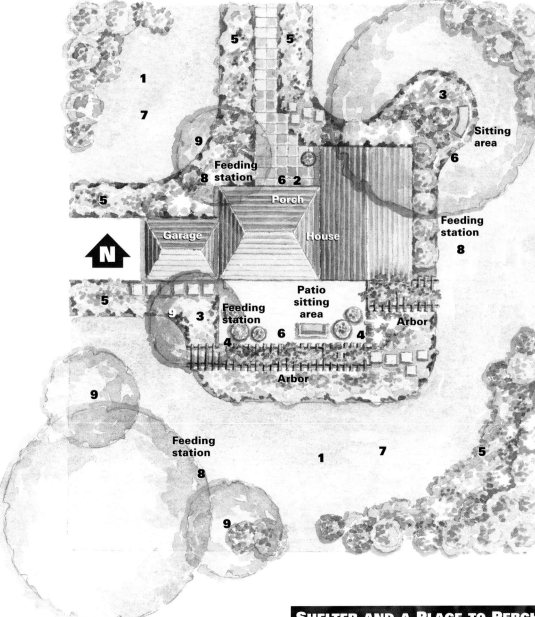

5 5

1

7

9

Feeding station
8

6 2

Porch

3

Sitting area

6

Feeding station
8

5

Garage

House

N

5

9

3

Feeding station

Patio sitting area

4

6

4

Arbor

Arbor

9

Feeding station

8

1

7

5

9

Remember these key points when making your yard friendly to hummingbirds:

1. Open lawn provides space for courtship display flights.

2. Nectar flowers on your porch bring fearless hummers up close.

3. Classic hostas and impatiens attract hummers to shady spots.

4. Plant flowering vines in pots and let them twine on an arbor around the patio or a railing around the deck.

5. Use plenty of red and red-orange flowers to catch the eye of nectar-seeking hummingbirds.

6. Watching hummingbirds is the payoff for your planting, so include several sitting areas in your yard.

7. When watering lawns, set the sprinkler on the finest mist to attract hummingbirds, which bathe on the wing.

8. Two or more feeding stations are better than one, because hummingbirds are often strongly territorial.

9. Colorful small trees, such as red buckeye, can be attractive to hummingbirds.

Hummingbirds are attracted to a garden that includes open space, because it allows them to move freely from one nectar source to another and practice their aerial displays. "Open" doesn't mean bare. Hummingbirds easily zip through space above flower beds, lawn, groundcovers, or patios.

Plan on about one-fourth of the yard shaded, one-fourth partially shaded, and the rest in open sun most of the day. Most hummingbird flowers grow best in sun, so the open space in your yard is ideal for flower beds. Curving beds allow hummingbirds to approach blooms from several sides. Keep shorter flowers in front of tall ones.

SHELTER AND A PLACE TO PERCH

Although hummingbirds may appear to be active every minute, they actually spend about four-fifths of each day perched quietly in trees or bushes. Every 10 to 15 minutes, the birds leave the perch to feed.

Males perch almost anywhere in the open—on twigs, clotheslines, and overhead wires. Females and immature birds are more likely to remain hidden within a tree, shrub, or vine. Hummingbirds roost at night until early dawn within the protective shelter of dense foliage.

Woody plants provide excellent shelter and perches. If space is limited, choose plants that do double duty as both food and shelter, such as citrus, cape honeysuckle, desert willow, weigela, flowering quince, and beauty bush.

CONTAINERS FOR HUMMINGBIRDS

Plants in containers are a quick and portable way to bring hummingbirds to your patio, deck, or veranda. Even the smallest garden has room for a hanging basket, clay pot, or window box. In a larger garden, containers provide variety and make the garden look more interesting by serving as a focal point. The burst of bloom will attract hummingbirds, who may even linger to nest in your hanging basket.

Many hummingbird flowers thrive in containers, including billowy blue catmint and elegant fuchsia. Australian fan flower and parrot's beak are trailing plants excellent for hanging baskets. Scented geraniums, with their wonderful fragrances, are a delight to humans as well as hummingbirds. Tropical plants such as coral fountain (*Russelia* spp.) and Chinese hibiscus (*Hibiscus rosa-sinensis*) are hummingbird magnets.

To make the most of a container garden, choose plants with long seasons of bloom and replace faded plants with fresh performers. Hummingbirds are not shy around humans, so be sure to place containers near favorite sitting spots or hang a basket at eye level, so you can enjoy the birds at close range.

Above: the cherry-colored flowers of geraniums, scarlet trumpets of Fuchsia × triphylla, *and spikes of red salvia show off in front of a red-leaf banana* (Ensete ventricosum 'Maurelii').

Above: A pink, blue, and white theme with, from left to right, Australian fan flower (Scaevola spp.), *pink and salmon scarlet sage* (Salvia splendens), *rose-scented geranium* (Pelargonium graveolens 'Grey Lady Plymouth'), *nutmeg-scented geranium* (Pelargonium 'Fragrans'), *dark and light blue edging lobelia* (Lobelia erinus), *and white Texas sage* (Salvia coccinea 'White Lady').

Overflowing with petunias, geraniums, and a curtain of feathery parrot's beak (Lotus berthelottii), *this basket has hummingbird appeal.*

HUMMINGBIRD PLANTS FOR HANGING BASKETS

Annual phlox (*Phlox drummondii*)
Australian fan flower (*Scaevola* spp.)
Begonia (*Begonia* spp.)
Cypress vine (*Ipomoea quamoclit*)
Edging lobelia (*Lobelia erinus*)
Fuchsia (*Fuchsia* spp.)
Geranium (*Pelargonium* spp.)
Impatiens (*Impatiens walleriana*)
Nasturtium (*Tropaeolum majus*)
Parrot's beak (*Lotus berthelottii*)
Petunia (*Petunia* spp.)
Spanish flag (*Ipomoea lobata*)

WINDOW BOXES FOR HUMMINGBIRDS

To hummingbirds, window boxes are much more than decoration; their colorful flowers promise accessible nectar. Window boxes are valuable to gardeners, too, because they expand space for gardening. Many flowers can be packed into a small area, there are few weeds, and the "garden" is quickly finished.

Plants used in hanging baskets are equally well-suited to window boxes. Taller and larger plants can also find a home here. Turn to scarlet sage (*Salvia splendens*) for months of beckoning red blossoms, or try its more relaxed-looking relative, Texas sage (*Salvia coccinea*), with an edging of blue lobelia (*Lobelia erinus*) or a trailing curtain of feathery-leaved parrot's beak. The classic combination of geraniums and petunias will also bring hummingbirds to your window.

Full-course meal in a box: fuchsia, cigar plant, and monkey flower accented by bold nasturtium leaves and red verbena.

Add hummingbird perennials, such as columbine, dwarf delphinium, and catmint, by popping them—in their plastic pots—into a window box when they're in flower. Then move them to the garden when they're finished blooming.

WINDOW BOX PLANTS FOR HUMMINGBIRDS

Annual phlox (*Phlox drummondii*)	Cigar plant (*Cuphea ignea*)	Geranium (*Pelargonium* × *hortorum*)	Rosemary (*Rosmarinus officinalis*)
Australian fan flower (*Scaevola* spp.)	Culinary sage (*Salvia officinalis*)	Impatiens (*Impatiens* spp.)	Scarlet sage (*Salvia splendens*)
Canary creeper (*Tropaeolum peregrinum*)	Delphinium (*Delphinium grandiflorum* 'Dwarf Blue Butterfly')	Nasturtium (*Tropaeolum majus*)	Scented geranium (*Pelargonium* spp.)
Catmint (*Nepeta* spp.)	Edging lobelia (*Lobelia erinus*)	Parrot's beak (*Lotus berthelottii*) Petunia (*Petunia* spp.)	Texas sage (*Salvia coccinea*)

FOUR-SEASON WINDOW BOXES

For nectar all year-round, plant these hummingbird-attracting flowers in your window boxes. Find plants in bud and bloom at garden centers or in the houseplant section of your nursery. (In cold-winter areas, fill the box with branches of pine, holly, or other greenery to keep them looking good in the off-season.)

Spring	Summer	Fall	Winter
Annual phlox (*Phlox drummondii*)	Australian fan flower (*Scaevola* spp.)	Cardinal flower (*Lobelia cardinalis*)	Dwarf citrus (*Citrus* spp.)
Catmint (*Nepeta* spp.)	Begonia (*Begonia* spp.)	Cigar plant (*Cuphea ignea*)	Fuchsia (*Fuchsia* spp.)
Columbine (*Aquilegia* spp.)	Canary creeper (*Tropaeolum peregrinum*)	Petunia (*Petunia* spp.)	Geranium (*Pelargonium* × *hortorum*)
Culinary sage (*Salvia officinalis*)	Dwarf delphinium (*Delphinium grandiflorum* 'Dwarf Blue Butterfly')	Scarlet sage (*Salvia splendens*)	Impatiens (*Impatiens walleriana*)
Fuchsia (*Fuchsia* spp.)	Edging lobelia (*Lobelia erinus*)	Scented geranium (*Pelargonium* spp.)	Rosemary (*Rosmarinus officinalis*)
	Geranium (*Pelargonium* × *hortorum*)	Texas sage (*Salvia coccinea*)	
	Impatiens (*Impatiens walleriana*)		
	Nasturtium (*Tropaeolum majus*)		
	Parrot's beak (*Lotus berthelottii*)		
	Petunia (*Petunia* spp.)		

WILDFLOWER GARDENS FOR HUMMINGBIRDS

Hummingbirds will visit nectar flowers no matter what style of garden they grow in, but if you like the natural look, your hummingbirds will find plenty of nectar in a wildflower garden. This type of garden has a more casual look than a traditional bed of annuals or perennials. Plants are arranged in a natural setting— a sunny meadow, a dry desert, a woodsy spot, a rocky outcrop— where they can spread and mingle as they would in nature.

For maximum hummingbird appeal, make sure to include red-flowering plants and those with tubular blossoms. Many native North American wildflowers attract hummingbirds, and their bloom periods coincide with the birds' life cycle. Some offer migrants nectar in early spring and fall, and others sustain the birds through nesting.

Many popular garden plants were once wildflowers, so they are equally at home in a wilder garden that resembles their natural origins. Columbine, for example, is easy to work into a natural setting, where it can spread in a meadow, among rocks, in desert areas, or along a stream. In the West, monkey flower (*Mimulus* spp.) grows well with little attention. Many residents of the Southwest position century plant (*Agave americana*) or ocotillo (*Fouquieria splendens*)— two of the most highly rated desert

Wildflowers provide nectar during critical migration times. Red-flowering currant, top, greets early spring migrants such as this Anna's Hummingbird. Below, a columbine tempts a Rufous.

hummingbird plants—to accent the lines of their ranch-style homes. In the East and Midwest, perennial cardinal flower (*Lobelia cardinalis*) is right at home beside a pool or stream, where it will supply nectar from summer into fall.

Plant wide sweeps of annual wildflowers, such as annual phlox or Indian paintbrush. Many will self-sow, giving you a self-renewing supply of hummingbird flowers. Include bee balm, delphinium, and other perennials in meadow gardens, or plant a hard-to-mow bank with penstemons and salvias. Wild flowering shrubs and trees, such as red-flowering currant (*Ribes sanguineum*), pinxterbloom azalea (*Rhododendron periclymenoides*), and the shrubby varieties of monkey flower (*Mimulus* spp.), are also gratifying when they're buzzing with hummingbirds.

WILDFLOWERS FOR HUMMINGBIRDS

Annual phlox (*Phlox drummondii*)
Bee balm (*Monarda* spp.)
California fuchsia (*Epilobium canum*)
Cardinal flower and great blue lobelia
    (*Lobelia cardinalis, L. siphilitica*)
Century plant (*Agave americana*)
Columbine (*Aquilegia* spp.)
Coral bell (*Heuchera* spp.)
Delphinium and larkspur (*Delphinium* spp.)
Fire pink and other pinks (*Silene* spp.)
Gilia (*Ipomopsis* spp.)
Indian paintbrush (*Castilleja* spp.)
Jewelweed (*Impatiens capensis*)
Maryland figwort (*Scrophularia marilandica*)
Monkey flower (*Mimulus* spp.)
Native honeysuckle (*Lonicera* spp.)
Ocotillo (*Fouquieria splendens*)
Penstemon (*Penstemon* spp.)
Purple four-o-clock (*Mirabilis multiflora*)
Red-flowering currant (*Ribes sanguineum*)
Sage; salvia (*Salvia* spp.)

At left is a spring welcome for early migrants with some favorite hummingbird native plants and wildflowers. Clockwise from upper right are: red-flowering currant, western columbine, Virginia bluebells, and a red buckeye tree.

WATER FOR HUMMINGBIRDS

The daily liquid intake of hummingbirds is as much as eight times their body weight. Much of this is in the form of nectar and sap from trees, but, like other birds, they drink water from whatever sources are available.

In early morning, after a heavy dew, or after a rain shower, hummingbirds may sip water or even splash in a water-filled leaf on a plant. These birds also have the charming habit of bathing on the wing. They often fly through fine spray from a waterfall. In the garden, you can attract them by supplying a sprinkler set to a fine mist for their bathing pleasure. Sometimes a hummingbird will fly through the spray as you hold a hose to water your plants. They loop back and forth through the water droplets, then retreat to a perch to shake and preen.

Water in a birdbath is normally much too deep for hummingbirds. But if you supply an elevated birdbath with very shallow water, hummingbirds may adopt it for their use. They usually avoid coming to the ground to drink or bathe.

Hummingbirds bathe in much the same way as other birds, ducking the head under and using the bill to flip water over the back. When bathing on the wing, they often wriggle in the spray. They will also dip down to water while in flight, barely touching the surface with their breast feathers. After a wetting, a hummingbird will go to a perch to shake off the water and preen its feathers.

Drops of water collected in the leaves of a fuchsia quench the thirst of an Anna's Hummingbird. Look for such behavior after a rain or after watering your garden.

Water is one of the few hummingbird essentials not produced by plants. Provide a source of water in your hummingbird garden, and the birds will reward you with their antics as they bathe and drink. During periods of drought, or in an area with long dry seasons, a sprinkler system can be just as attractive to hummingbirds as the finest nectar flowers. Once they discover a regular source of water, they'll return day after day.

BEST SPRINKLERS FOR HUMMINGBIRDS

Tiny hummingbirds prefer fine droplets of water to bathe in, so look for a hose nozzle or sprinkler that breaks up the stream of water into as fine a mist as possible.

Sprinklers, either oscillating or stationary, work well for hummingbird showers. Look for one that can deliver a fine, low-pressure spray of water; the water head should have many tiny holes. Aim the sprinkler over an open area of lawn or low plants so that hummingbirds have a clear flight path as they buzz in and out of the spray.

If you live in a hot-summer area, you may want to invest in a misting system designed for cooling patios and outdoor living areas. The path of its ultrafine spray is wide enough for a dozen hummingbirds to enjoy at the same time. Or you can buy a single small mist outlet designed specifically for hummingbirds. The Whispering Waters Mini-Mister, marketed by Duncraft (see page 33), is simple to fasten to a tree or trellis and can be connected to a timer.

Whatever sprinkler you buy, be sure to mount your hummingbird shower where you can have a clear view of the birds cavorting in the spray.

Like kids at play, a trio of immature Rufous Hummingbirds splashes in a sprinkler.

HUMMINGBIRD FEEDERS: SELECTION AND PLACEMENT

1. *This feeder's long perches allow more birds to wait their turn.*
2. *A feeder with a horizontal reservoir is easy to clean and prevents drips.*
3. *This popular four-perch model has yellow bee guards to keep out insect pests.*
4. *A gracefully styled feeder ornaments your garden.*
5. *A large feeder requires less frequent refills.*
6. *A flower feeder is fun for children to "plant."*

F eeding hummingbirds is a rewarding hobby. Best of all is seeing hummingbirds up close as they come to drink. A few minutes invested in cleaning and refilling feeders pays off in hours of pleasure.

CHOOSING A FEEDER

Hummingbirds are easy to please and always hungry. They will come to any feeder that allows space for maneuvering and provides suitable openings into which to thrust their bills. Hummingbirds often zero in on a new feeder almost instantly, but if they are not accustomed to visiting your neighborhood, it can take months for the birds to discover a feeder. Feeder populations peak during spring and fall migration.

Store-bought hummingbird feeders are inexpensive and durable. Start with a small model that accommodates three birds. As the population grows, you can add more feeders, including large-capacity models that you won't have to refill as often.

You can also make your own feeder. Any container that will hold water can become a hummingbird feeder. Drinking bottles for small pets, which consist of inverted glass bottles with a glass tube at the bottom, are a low-cost alternative. Even a test tube or jar hung at an angle will attract hummingbirds. Dab red fingernail polish around the opening or attach a red ribbon or an artificial flower to advertise your homemade feeder.

PLACING FEEDERS

Place your first feeder where hummingbirds are most likely to see it—near flowers and in the sun. Later, after hummingbirds are in the habit of visiting, you can move it to a spot that gives you a better view. Putting a feeder in view also helps you monitor it for refills and cleaning.

Windows are hazards to hummingbirds, so place feeders either a safe distance away from the house or very close to a window. Birds coming to feeders 15 to 20 feet away are less likely to fly into the glass. If your site is less than 15 feet from a window, move the feeder to within a few inches of the glass or use one that attaches to the glass with suction cups.

Hummingbirds spend a large part of their time perched in a tree or shrub. Here, safe from predators, they wait until it is necessary to fly out in search of food. The closer they

EASY TO CLEAN, EASY TO FILL

Hummingbirds aren't particular about feeder design, but ease of filling and cleaning is important to those who maintain the feeders. Before you buy, give all the feeders a workout as if you were actually using them. Unhook the feeder or unscrew the cap and imagine that the reservoir is full of sugar water. Sugar water is sticky stuff, so select a feeder that you can take down and refill without messy spills. Consider also how you will go about cleaning it. Will you have to wiggle a bottle brush into nooks and crannies, or can you twist the feeder apart for a fast wipe-down? Are the feeding holes easy to clean? One last recommendation: Be sure the feeder you choose gives you a clear view of the liquid within. Opaque ceramic or art glass feeders may be beautiful, but you won't be able to tell when they need refilling, and empty feeders will frustrate hummingbirds.

Once hummingbirds discover your nectar feeders, they will return daily, perhaps bringing their young once they leave the nest. During migration, traffic at nectar feeders often increases. Position feeders with safety in mind, and make sure you enjoy a clear view of the customers.

are to a food supply, the less energy they will expend and the shorter the distance they need to fly if danger looms. Put your feeders within 10 to 15 feet of the nearest cover. If the feeders are much farther away from cover, hummingbirds will be reluctant to visit them.

Partial shade is best. Feeders that have openings below the reservoir depend on a vacuum to hold the liquid in place. In hot weather, they may drip when the air above the liquid heats, expands, and pushes water out of the openings. A shady spot keeps feeders cool and minimizes dripping. (Feeders that have holes above the reservoir do not drip.) Shade also slows down spoilage of the solution. However, a hummingbird shines in full glory only in sun. A reasonable solution is to place feeders where they will be in the shade most of the day yet in the sun for at least a few hours.

UNINVITED GUESTS

Drawn by a universal taste for sweets, other visitors besides hummingbirds come to nectar feeders—lizards, bats, opossums, raccoons, foxes, squirrels, chipmunks, and many songbirds.

Other birds are the most common interlopers at hummingbird feeders. Orioles, accustomed to visiting flowers for nectar, are among the most persistent of the bird visitors, followed by house finches, warblers, chickadees, woodpeckers, and many others. The total number of bird species so far reported at nectar feeders has reached 60.

Watching these guests can be entertaining. Discouraging them can be difficult. If orioles are your problem, supply them with their own specially designed feeders. Place a few new feeders, without perches, for your hummingbirds. If all else fails, remove the feeders. Hummingbirds will still visit your yard to seek nectar at flowers, and in a few weeks you can try slipping the feeders back in.

A lack of perches doesn't keep this determined Acorn Woodpecker from satisfying its sweet tooth.

HUMMINGBIRD FEEDERS: CARE

Casual mixing of sugar-water solutions can result in a stronger or weaker ratio than the recommended 4:1. It's best to measure sugar first, but if you forget, use the displacement method: The water level will rise by about ¼ cup for each half cup of sugar added.

fatal fungal disease of the tongue, or artificial sweeteners, which provide no calories. Red food coloring is unnecessary, because the red plastic on the feeder is attraction enough, and the food coloring may be potentially harmful.

To make nectar, stir sugar and water in a pan over low heat and bring to a boil. Boil for 2 minutes. Boiling kills mold spores and bacteria and, through evaporation, reduces any chlorine or fluorine that may be in the water and may cause hummingbirds to avoid the feeder. Avoid overboiling, which can make the solution stronger than a 1:4 ratio. After the solution cools, fill the feeders. Store extra nectar in the refrigerator.

REDUCING COMPETITION

Hummingbirds chase and challenge one another whether they feed at flowers or sugar-water feeders. Sometimes an unusually aggressive bird (often an adult male) attempts to keep all the others away by watching from a prominent perch and immediately giving chase as soon as another bird appears. If many birds are visiting a feeder, the bully may find it impossible to keep them all away. While it is giving chase to one bird, the others are able to feed at least briefly without being molested.

The best strategy is to keep your feeders well apart. Add other feeders on different sides of the house, and use vegetation to hide one feeder from another. The most effective plan might be to provide the aggressive bird with a feeder of its own that is at some distance from the other feeders.

NECTAR

The standard solution for feeding hummingbirds consists of 1 part white sugar to 4 parts water, which closely approximates the strength of flower nectar. Stronger concentrations have been found to adversely affect the livers of captive birds; weaker concentrations are less attractive. Do not substitute honey, which spoils much more quickly and contains a bacteria that causes a

DETERRING PESTS

Ants, bees, wasps, and their close relatives visit feeders for the same reason as hummingbirds—for the sweet-tasting solution. If overly numerous they keep hummingbirds away and drain the feeders. They are also a nuisance to gardeners.

To deter ants, block their approach route. Coating the feeder support with petroleum jelly is effective. So are water-filled moats, which are often attached to commercial feeders or which you can fashion yourself with a bit of ingenuity.

Bee guards—small screens that come with many commercial

feeders and fit over the feeding ports— prevent bees and their relatives from reaching the nectar, which with their long, slender bills is still accessible to hummingbirds. Clean the guards frequently.

You can also discourage bees and wasps by smearing the surfaces around the feeding openings with slippery substances such as petroleum jelly, salad oil, or mineral oil, which will prevent the insects from getting a foothold. Apply sparingly, taking care not to let any get in the feeder and contaminate the solution. Reapply as needed.

Do not use pesticides. Both hummingbirds and the small insects they need for food could be adversely affected.

CLEANING THE FEEDER

Clean your feeders at least every three days in hot weather and every six or seven days in cool weather. If you are lax about cleaning, the solution soon becomes cloudy and eventually begins to ferment. Careful examination will reveal small black specks in the liquid and mold beginning to form on the inside of the plastic or glass reservoir holding the solution. These are danger signals. Harmful bacteria and mold present health risks to hummingbirds and can kill them.

Make it a routine to take down the feeders every few days for cleaning. Here's how:

1. Empty any leftover solution and rinse in warm water.

2. Add a splash of vinegar and grains of uncooked rice to the rinse and shake the feeder vigorously to dislodge any mold in the container.

3. Empty the feeder and rinse it again with warm water.

4. If some mold remains, scrub it off with a small percolator brush or bottle brush.

A common complaint among novices is that the birds are ignoring their feeders. Often the reason is that the solution has become sour and, as a result, the birds are not drinking it. When you start a feeding program, pour only a small amount of sugar water into a feeder. In this way, you will waste only a little when the time comes to empty the feeder and add more solution.

Easy to maneuver into tight spaces, a bottle brush makes quick work of mold scum. Rinse the feeder thoroughly to remove all traces of dish detergent before refilling. If you refill daily, rinse out the feeder with clean water between uses, and scrub thoroughly every few days.

FOR ADDITIONAL INFORMATION ON HUMMINGBIRDS

Field guides for hummingbird identification:
A Field Guide to the Birds: A Completely New Guide to All the Birds of Eastern and Central North America, by Roger Tory Peterson (Houghton Mifflin, 1998)
A Field Guide to Western Birds, by Roger Tory Peterson (Houghton Mifflin, 1990)
Field Guide to the Birds of North America, by Jon L. Dunn (National Geographic Society, 1999)
National Audubon Society Field Guide to North American Birds: Eastern Region, by John Bull (Knopf, 1994)
National Audubon Society Field Guide to North American Birds: Western Region, by Miklos Udvardy, John Farrand, Jr. (Knopf, 1994)

To join a group of hummingbird enthusiasts, contact:
The Hummingbird Society, P.O. Box 394, Newark, DE 19715. Online: www.hummingbird.org
The National Audubon Society, 700 Broadway, New York, NY 10003. Online: www.audubon.org. This is a good place to learn more about hummingbirds as well as

other birds and conservation issues. Check the phone book or call a nearby nature center to find your local chapter.
To buy nectar feeders, misters, and other supplies by mail, contact:
Droll Yankees Inc., 27 Mill Rd., Foster, RI 02825. Online: www.drollyankees.com
Duncraft, 102 Fisherville Rd., Concord, NH 03303. Online: www.duncraft.com
Wild Birds Unlimited, 270 stores nationwide. Online: www.wbu.com

To make your yard more inviting to hummingbirds and other birds, participate in the Backyard Wildlife Habitat Program of the National Wildlife Federation, designed for properties from windowsill-size to acres. Your yard can be certified if it meets requirements for food, water, and shelter. Contact:
The National Wildlife Federation, Backyard Wildlife Habitat Program, 8925 Leesburg Pike, Vienna, VA 22184-0001. Online: www.nwf.org/habitats

GALLERY OF HUMMINGBIRD PLANTS

Bring the life and color of hummingbirds to your yard by filling your gardens with the plants in this gallery. You'll find many perennials, plus an intriguing selection of vines and shrubs. Many are American natives, ideal for hummingbirds because they provide nectar during spring and fall migration times, and are easily adapted to life in the garden, where they are generally trouble-free. Notice the many red and red-orange blossoms, the colors that hummingbirds find most appealing. You'll also find all the information you need to help you decide which plants are best for your conditions and climate, including the hardiness zones for each perennial. Consult the map on page 92 to find the USDA hardiness zone for your area. On pages 42 and 43 you will find additional plants attractive to hummingbirds, listed by region.

AQUILEGIA SPP.

ak-wee-LEE-jee-uh

Columbine

- Perennial
- Long-spurred blossoms in red, yellow, blue, white, and pink to deep purple
- 1 to 2 feet high

Golden columbine (Aquilegia chrysantha) *patronized by a Black-chinned Hummingbird.*

24" / 12"

- Spring to summer bloom
- Zones 3 to 9, depending on species

Columbines are hummingbird magnets. Beautiful in the garden, their striking spurred flowers have an eye-catching shape that is tailor-made for long, skinny hummingbird bills. They bloom for several weeks, a longer period than most perennials. Many are American natives, from such diverse habitats as the rainy Northwest, dry desert, high mountains, and eastern woodlands. Non-native species and hybrids also attract hummingbirds. Deeply divided foliage similar to maidenhair fern adds delicate texture to the garden.

CULTURE: Plant columbines in light to moderate shade in well-drained soil. They are easy to grow from seed and self-sow moderately. They combine well with other plants for a natural effect in borders, rock gardens, cottage gardens, and shade gardens. Leaf miners may leave scribbled tan lines in foliage but will not kill the plant.

RECOMMENDED SPECIES AND CULTIVARS: Any columbine is a good columbine as far as hummingbirds are concerned. Thirty species are native to North America, so there are plenty to sample. Try butter-yellow golden columbine (*A. chrysantha*), clear blue Rocky Mountain columbine (*A. caerulea*), and the two similar red wild columbines, *A. formosa* from the West and *A. canadensis* from the East. 'McKana's Giants', 'Crimson Star', and snow white 'Silver Queen' are a few of the many excellent cultivars.

BUDDLEIA DAVIDII

BUD-lee-uh duh-VID-ee-aye

Butterfly bush

Butterfly bush (Buddleia davidii) *brings months of bloom, irresistible to hummingbirds and butterflies.*

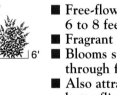
8' / 6'

- Free-flowering shrub 6 to 8 feet tall
- Fragrant
- Blooms summer through fall
- Also attracts butterflies
- Zones 5 to 9

A summer-long banquet for hummingbirds and butterflies, this shrub, sometimes called summer lilac, sends out arching branches with a fountain of purple, lavender, pink, or white blooms. Give it a place of honor in your garden, and allow room to walk around it to get a close-up view of feeding hummingbirds and butterflies.

CULTURE: Plant butterfly bush in full sun in average, well-drained soil. It also thrives in lean and light soils. Native to China and Japan, this shrub has naturalized in North America in some areas. Cut entire plant to ground in late winter for more vigorous growth and abundant summer flowers. Propagates easily from 8- to 12-inch cuttings pushed into moist soil.

RECOMMENDED CULTIVARS: The unimproved species is an excellent garden plant. 'Black Knight' has dramatic deep purple-black flowers. 'Nanho Purple' is a dwarf version, good in small gardens. White cultivars seem to be less appealing to hummingbirds.

CAMPSIS RADICANS

KAMP-sis RAD-ih-kanz

Trumpet creeper

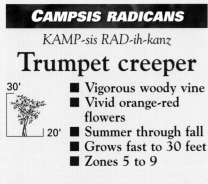

30'
20'

- Vigorous woody vine
- Vivid orange-red flowers
- Summer through fall
- Grows fast to 30 feet
- Zones 5 to 9

This perennial vine is noted for its vigor. Support it with a strong arbor or trellis, or grow it along a wall or sturdy fence. In the right site, trumpet vine is a beauty, with bright flowers shining against deep green foliage. Long, dangling seedpods

keep the plant's twisting silhouette interesting in winter.

CULTURE: Plant in sun to shade in average soil. This Southeast native needs no fertilizing or other special attention to look good in the garden. A vigorous plant with rampant growth, trumpet vine requires strict control, especially in southern gardens, where *C. grandiflora* is a better-behaved choice. Snip off volunteer shoots as they arise from the roots. Avoid planting *C. radicans* near wooden structures, where its strong stems can infiltrate between boards.

RECOMMENDED CULTIVARS: The unimproved species is highly attractive to hummingbirds. Yellow-

flowered 'Flava' and the large-flowered hybrid *C.* × *tagliabuana* 'Mme. Galen' are also good choices. *Campsis grandiflora*, a Chinese species of trumpet vine, has huge orange flowers that shine like a beacon to hummingbirds.

Trumpet vine (Campsis radicans) sounds a clarion call to a female Ruby-throated Hummingbird.

CASTILLEJA SPP.

cas-tih-LAY-uh

Indian paintbrush

24"
12"

- Annual, biennial, and perennial plants
- Bright blooms spring through summer
- 6 inches to 3 feet tall
- Best as self-sowing wildflower
- Zones 4 to 8, depending on species

A common sight in the West, Indian paintbrushes usually do not thrive outside their natural region, because many are semi-parasitic on

roots of native grasses. Most species are native to the western mountains and Great Plains.

CULTURE: If you live where the plants are native, enjoy wild plants that show up on their own, and sow seed in average soil in a natural meadow garden. Include native grasses and avoid weeding, which may disturb roots. Once established, often self-sows. Transplanting is usually unsuccessful.

RECOMMENDED SPECIES: *Castilleja coccinea*, an annual or biennial, is a beautiful and widespread scarlet species, good for gardens from eastern Canada through New England, south to Florida, and west to Oklahoma.

Downy painted cup (*C. sessiliflora*) thrives in the upper Midwest, south to Texas, and westward. Giant painted cup, *C. miniata*, a perennial, is a spectacular western wildflower that reaches 3 feet.

Castilleja coccinea is an Indian paintbrush native to the Midwest.

CHILOPSIS LINEARIS

chih-LOP-sis lih-nee-AIR-iss

Desert willow

25'
25'

- Small tree to 25 feet with striking silhouette
- Willowlike leaves and clouds of pink-lavender flowers
- Excellent for dry and desert gardens
- Early summer through fall bloom
- Zones 7 to 10

Not a willow at all but a relative of trumpet vine and cross vine,

this interesting southwestern native tree is appealing in all seasons. In winter, it reveals twisting, twiggy branches. Perfect for a small or large garden; plant penstemons and other drought-tolerant plants beneath its airy branches. Bright spring green foliage makes dry gardens look lush.

CULTURE: Plant in extremely well-drained soil; add sand if needed to lighten the texture. Deep roots need no extra watering. Plant in groups or hedges or use a single tree as an eye-catching accent. Clusters of seedpods are held through winter.

RECOMMENDED CULTIVARS: 'Barranca' ('Barranco') is more upright than the usual wide-branched form; its flowers are deep

lavender and appealing to hummingbirds. 'Hope', a white-flowered cultivar, has less initial attraction for hummingbirds than the unimproved pink- or purple-flowered species.

Desert willow (Chilopsis linearis) offers beautiful greenery and abundant nectar for a dry garden.

CLEOME SPP.

klee-OH-me

Spider flower

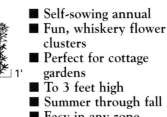

4'

1'

- Self-sowing annual
- Fun, whiskery flower clusters
- Perfect for cottage gardens
- To 3 feet high
- Summer through fall
- Easy in any zone

Spider flower (Cleome hassleriana) is easy to grow from seed, in single colors or a mix.

As easy to grow as marigolds, spider flowers bloom for weeks in the garden, providing plenty of nectar throughout the summer and during fall hummingbird migration. Long, thin stamens that protrude from the flowers and slim, elongated seedpods, which appear from the base of the flower cluster while upper flowers are still budding and blooming, give the plant its common name. Watch the delicate flowers quiver in the breeze that a hummingbird creates. Several species hail from South America, where hummingbirds abound.

RECOMMENDED SPECIES AND CULTIVARS: Tall, showy *Cleome hassleriana* is deservedly popular with gardeners and hummingbirds; its flowers are pink, rosy purple, or white. Try intensely colored 'Rose Queen'. Two North American natives, the Rocky Mountain bee plant (*C. serrulata*), a species with pink-purple flowers, and the yellow bee plant (*C. lutea*), attract a multitude of nectar-seeking insects as well as hummingbirds.

DELPHINIUM SPP.

del-FIN-ee-um

Delphinium

5'

3'

- Clear, intense colors
- 1 to 6 feet tall
- Spring to summer
- Zones 3 to 10; annuals all zones

Red delphinium (Delphinium cardinale) attracts an Allen's Hummingbird.

From delicate species to tall hybrids, the elegant spikes of delphiniums make a striking garden centerpiece. The spur of the flower holds nectar at the ready for long-billed hummingbirds, which will linger for minutes at each plant. All colors are attractive to hummingbirds.

CULTURE: Sow seeds or settle started plants into fertile, well-drained soil in full sun; a few species, including the native *D. trolliifolium*, flourish in shade.

Cut off faded flower spike for more side blooms and a longer season.

RECOMMENDED SPECIES AND CULTIVARS: Single blossoms rather than double-flowered varieties are most attractive to hummingbirds. Red *Delphinium cardinale*, a native of California and Mexico, and its cultivar 'Beverly Hills', are absolute magnets. The tall 'Pacific Giants' are spectacular, as are the shorter 'Magic Fountains'. Annual delphinium, commonly called larkspur, was once classified with the genus *Delphinium* but has been renamed as *Consolida ambigua*; it is simple to grow from seed and perfect for a casual garden where it can self-sow.

EPILOBIUM CANUM SSP. CANUM

ep-uh-LO-bee-um KAY-num subspecies KAY-num

California fuchsia

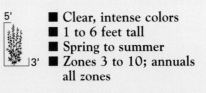

1'

2'

- Spreading perennial
- Blooms midsummer to frost
- Overwinter cuttings
- 1 foot tall
- Zones 4 to 10

California fuchsia (Epilobium canum ssp. canum) lives up to its nickname of "hummingbird flower."

Hummingbirds mob California fuchsia, especially during migration in fall. Also known as hummingbird flower, this spreading perennial is perfect for covering a sunny bank, in natural plantings, or in a gravelly patch beside the driveway. It is one of the few western native plants that provides outstanding late-season color.

CULTURE: This California native demands excellent drainage.

It spreads by underground runners, but is seldom invasive. Start from seed, cuttings, or runners, or settle a nursery plant in sharply drained soil in full sun. It thrives in dry-summer areas and drought. Cut it back hard in late fall for vigor.

RECOMMENDED SPECIES AND CULTIVARS: Formerly known as *Zauschneria californica*, this species has now been moved to a genus that includes fireweed (*Epilobium angustifolium*), another spreading perennial with hummingbird appeal. A close relative, *Epilobium septentrionale* (formerly *Zauschneria septentrionalis*) and its cultivars 'Mattole' and 'Brilliant Smith', are also excellent for hummingbirds.

FUCHSIA MAGELLANICA

FEW-shyuh ma-jeh-LAN-ih-kuh

Fuchsia

6'

4'

- Shrub, usually about 6 feet tall
- Covered in dangling "earring" blossoms
- A hummingbird may claim shrub as territory
- Long bloom period
- Zones 7 to 10; worth a try in zone 6

Available in many shapes, sizes, and colors, fuchsias of all kinds are manna to hummingbirds. Most are hardy only in frost-free areas, but this species is a cold-tolerant shrub that can be grown in a wide area. Use it as a single specimen, in beds and borders, or as a hedge.

CULTURE: Plant in full sun to part shade, in well-drained, average soil. If top growth is killed by a cold snap, cut back to ground level in late winter for quick regrowth and bloom the same year. Some tender fuchsias are grown as annuals. Cuttings of all types root easily in moist soil.

RECOMMENDED SPECIES AND CULTIVARS: The species is just fine with hummingbirds. Other more tender cultivars also are attractive to hummingbirds. Try them in hanging baskets, as edging along a walk, or atop a wall, where they can dangle their blossoms at eye level. The hybrid cultivar 'Gartenmeister Bonstedt' bears orange-red trumpets on erect plants.

Fuchsia magellanica *has showy-leaved cultivars (this one is 'Aurea'), but its flowers are main attractions.*

HEUCHERA SANGUINEA

HEW-ker-a san-GWIN-ee-a

Coral bells

20"

20"

- Sprays of tiny blossoms above leaves
- Southwestern native
- Blooms in spring; may rebloom later
- Zones 4 to 9

The parent of many modern coral bells cultivars, this plant hails from the rocky deserts of Arizona and New Mexico, south to Mexico, but flourishes in the garden as well. The big flush of bloom comes in spring, but new bloom stalks may appear for months. Flowers are held on bare stems 6 inches to a foot or more above the low, leafy clump, so the plant is perfect for the front of the garden.

CULTURE: Start seeds in pots, or settle plants into well-drained soil, in sun to part shade. Prone to heaving from the ground during freeze-thaw cycles; push back in with your hands if necessary.

RECOMMENDED SPECIES AND CULTIVARS: Coral bells is an all-American plant, with species growing wild from coast to coast. All heuchera flowers attract hummingbirds, whether the blooms are blazing red (*H. sanguinea, H.* × *brizoides*) or white, pink, or greenish, as in *H. americana, H. maxima,* and *H. micrantha*. Even the dramatic purple-leaved cultivars, such as 'Palace Purple', have flowers with hummingbird appeal.

Coral bells, an American wildflower, has become a garden standard. This one is* Heuchera sanguinea *'Firebird'.

IPOMOPSIS SPP.

i-po-MOP-sis

Gilia

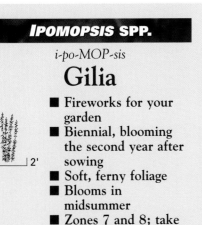

6'

2'

- Fireworks for your garden
- Biennial, blooming the second year after sowing
- Soft, ferny foliage
- Blooms in midsummer
- Zones 7 and 8; take a chance in Zone 6

Skyrocket is another common name for scarlet gilia, a stunning plant that will stop passing humans and hummingbirds in their tracks. In its first year, this biennial produces an attractive clump of delicate, filmy foliage. But the following year, it shoots skyward into a 6-foot column topped by a crown of brilliant red trumpets. Its height makes it easily visible to hummingbirds, whether in its native Southeast and Texas haunts or in your garden.

CULTURE: Sow seeds in well-drained soil in full sun. Drought-tolerant. Transplanting is almost always unsuccessful. With luck, the plants will self-sow.

RECOMMENDED SPECIES: *Ipomopsis rubra* may vary in height from 3 to 6 feet, but it is always a stunner. Shorter *I. aggregata*, native to the West and Northwest, has several stems instead of a single skyrocket.

Gilia (*Ipomopsis rubra*) advertises nectar with a show of fireworks atop tall stems.

LOBELIA CARDINALIS

lo-BEE-ee-uh kar-di-NAH-lis

Cardinal flower

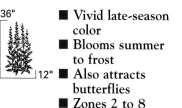
36"
12"

- ■ Vivid late-season color
- ■ Blooms summer to frost
- ■ Also attracts butterflies
- ■ Zones 2 to 8

A native wildflower of shaded and sunny streamsides and wet places, cardinal flower thrives just as well in the garden, with or without extra moisture. It begins blooming in midsummer and continues while hummingbirds are migrating to winter residences. The plant gets its common name not from the bird but from the color of the robes of church cardinals.

Cardinal flower (Lobelia cardinalis) draws a female Ruby-throated Hummingbird in late summer.

CULTURE: Settle plants in gardens or around pools and ponds in full sun to partial shade. Plants may decline after a few years; start cuttings in late spring to ensure a continual supply.

RECOMMENDED CULTIVARS: Although breeders have turned their attention to cardinal flower and its relative great blue lobelia (*Lobelia siphilitica*), both of these native plants have clearer colors and often more attractive shapes than cultivars such as 'Ruby Slippers' (a wine red) or 'Pink Flamingo'. Both species are equally attractive to hummingbirds, although they will find cardinal flower first because of its red color.

LONICERA SPP.

loh-NISS-er-uh

Honeysuckle

15'
10'

- ■ Vines or shrubs
- ■ Abundant flowers in red or yellow
- ■ Use for height in a small or large garden
- ■ Choose noninvasive varieties
- ■ Spring to summer bloom
- ■ Zones 4 to 8

Native honeysuckles and hybrids are well-behaved garden plants, unlike the rampant Japanese honeysuckle (*L. japonica*), which has swamped gardens and woods in many areas. Hummingbirds visit the blossoms daily, dipping their bills deep for nectar.

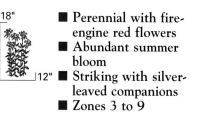

Lonicera sempervirens 'Magnifica' gets rave reviews from an Anna's Hummingbird.

CULTURE: Plant in sun to part shade in appropriate soil for the species. Woodland types grow best in a moist, mulched site; natives of the Southwest thrive in dry soils.

RECOMMENDED SPECIES AND CULTIVARS: Vivid, deep red trumpet honeysuckle (*Lonicera sempervirens*) is one of the best, reaching 10 to 15 feet tall. *L. arizonica* is a shrubby honeysuckle from the Southwest with red-and-orange flowers. Hybrids include *L.* × *brownii* and its popular cultivar 'Dropmore Scarlet'. Another fine hybrid is *L.* × *heckrottii* and its cultivar 'Goldflame', whose flowers have pinkish-purple exteriors with yellow inside.

LYCHNIS CHALCEDONICA

LICK-nis chal-seh-DON-ih-kuh

Maltese cross

18"
12"

- ■ Perennial with fire-engine red flowers
- ■ Abundant summer bloom
- ■ Striking with silver-leaved companions
- ■ Zones 3 to 9

A dramatic spot of color in a perennial garden, Maltese cross forms a loose clump of leafy, 18-inch-tall stems topped with clusters of up to 50 flowers. Thanks to its origins in Russia, this plant is gratifyingly cold-hardy. It is an excellent choice for hummingbird gardens in northern areas.

CULTURE: Start seeds in pots, or settle plants in full sun. Needs well-

Maltese cross (Lychnis chalcedonica) keeps hummingbirds lingering at its abundant flowers.

drained soil but suffers in drought. Add compost or manure to soil to improve water retention, and apply mulch to further conserve moisture.

RECOMMENDED SPECIES AND CULTIVARS: A guaranteed hummingbird attracter, *Lychnis chalcedonica* needs no improvement from its species form. The double-flowered 'Flore Plena' is less appealing to hummingbirds. *Lychnis* × *arkwrightii*, a hybrid similar to *L. chalcedonica* that is best treated as an annual, is available in a dwarf form, as well as the 18-inch-tall 'Vesuvius', with orange-red flowers and dark foliage. Biennial or short-lived perennial rose campion (*L. coronaria*) has rose-red flowers.

MIMULUS SPP.

MIM-yew-luss

Monkey flower

24"
18"

- Native annuals, perennials, and shrubs
- Excellent in moist areas
- Long bloom, spring through late summer
- Zones 7 to 9; annuals all zones

These mostly American natives are abundant in the West, with many species reaching peak bloom when hummingbirds are nesting or traveling. Although unfamiliar to many American gardeners, monkey flowers and their hybrids are well-known in European gardens. **CULTURE:** Sow seeds or plant in full sun to shade, depending on species, in moisture-retentive soil, such as the edges or crevices of water features. Many species also thrive in average garden conditions, so don't be afraid to experiment. **RECOMMENDED SPECIES AND CULTIVARS:** With 150 species, nearly all native to the Americas, monkey flowers are fun getting to know. Try M. *cardinalis*, a bright scarlet, or its cultivars 'Orange Perfection' and pink 'Roseus'. M. *lewisii* is another red, sometimes deep pink, species. Spectacular M. *aurantiacus*, or orange bush monkey flower, is a native western shrub. Blue M. *ringens* is an easy eastern species.

Orange bush monkey flower (Mimulus aurantiacus) *blooms spring through summer.*

MONARDA SPP.

mo-NAR-duh DI-di-ma

Bee balm

30"
18"

- Fast-spreading perennial
- Deliciously scented foliage, good for tea
- Blooms in summer
- 2 to 3 feet tall
- Zones 4 to 7

This unusual flower from shady American streamsides and open woods is a longtime garden favorite for attracting hummingbirds. The blossoms are made up of many individual tubular flowers. Plant near a garden bench so you can admire hummingbirds as they work their way around each blossom. **CULTURE:** Place plants in full sun to part shade in average soil, or in wet places. Mildew may disfigure foliage but is not fatal. A member of the mint family, bee balm spreads fast by underground runners but is not difficult to get back in bounds if necessary. Replant or give extra runners to gardening friends. **RECOMMENDED SPECIES AND CULTIVARS:** Pink M. *fistulosa*, dotted white and purple M. *citriodora*, and purplish M. *punctata* are all appealing to hummingbirds, although the red-flowered M. *didyma* gets top honors for reeling them in. 'Cambridge Scarlet' is an ideal cultivar for hummingbirds. Others expand the color choices: violet-pink 'Prairie Night'; white 'Snow Queen'; deep purplish 'Bluestocking'; and 'Croftway Pink'.

Pink bee balm (Monarda fistulosa) *attracts any nearby hummingbird, including this Broad-tailed male.*

NEPETA X FAASSENII

NEP-eh-tuh fa-SEN-ee-eye

Catmint

18"
18"

- Relaxed perennial for edging
- Billows of blue flowers
- Aromatic, silvery foliage
- Spring through summer bloom
- Zones 3 to 9

With its thousands of small, tubular flowers, catmint keeps hummingbirds busy taking short sips of nectar or sampling tiny insects also attracted to the blooms. A beautiful plant to combine with almost any other perennial, catmint is especially valuable for softening spiky forms, such as iris, and providing gentle, cooling color next to strong reds, oranges, or yellows. It also grows well in containers, making it a good plant for tempting hummingbirds to the patio or deck. **CULTURE:** Plant in full sun in well-drained soil rich in organic matter. Cut back plants in late winter to promote vigorous new growth. **RECOMMENDED CULTIVARS:** 'Blue Wonder', like all catmints, is extremely generous with its flowers, bearing clouds of blue for weeks. 'Blue Dwarf' is compact; 'Six Hills Giant' offers long sprays of blossoms. 'Souvenir d'Andre Chaudron' is a taller, more erect plant with large flowers of rich blue.

Upright catmint (Nepeta × faassenii 'Souvenir d'Andre Chaudron') *offers a good contrast to red and orange.*

PENSTEMON SPP.

PEN-steh-mon

Penstemon

30"
18"

- Perennials and shrubs
- Open spikes of tubular blossoms in red, blue, purple, pink, white
- Drought-tolerant
- Blooms spring, summer, or fall, depending on species
- Zones 3 to 10

Nearly all penstemons are native to the Americas, and most are found in the West and Southwest, where hummingbirds abound. Ranging from firecracker red to icy blue, they cling to rocky ledges and spring up from arroyos, carpet meadows, and brighten swamps and prairies.

There is sure to be a penstemon that fits your garden, since there are nearly 200 species in the genus with widely varied cultural requirements. Modern hybrids seem to be more adaptable to garden life than species grown outside their natural area.

CULTURE: Top-notch drainage is the key to success with penstemons, except for a few species, including Gulf Coast penstemon (*P. tenuis*). Most need full sun; a few tolerate light shade. Nearly all species like plenty of elbow room; crowding them among other plants may lead to a quick demise.

RECOMMENDED SPECIES AND CULTIVARS: Any penstemon is a good penstemon for hummingbirds. Red and orange species, highly attractive to hummingbirds, include *P. centranthifolius*, with vivid orange flowers; *P. barbatus*, or beardlip penstemon, with bright red blossoms; *P. corymbosus*, a brick red shrub type; and *P. eatonii*, scarlet firecracker, whose name says it all. Many penstemon cultivars are available, including *P. barbatus* 'Prairie Fire'; *P. digitalis* 'Husker Red', a cultivar with moody, deep red foliage; and *P. strictus* 'Bandera'. A sampling of hybrids hints at the wide color selection: 'Rose Elf', 'Blue Midnight', 'Schooley's Yellow', 'Grape Tart', and 'Cherry Glow'.

Penstemon barbatus 'Praecox Nana Rondo', *top;* P. whippleanus, *with Rufous Hummingbird male, above.*

Scarlet firecracker (P. eatonii) *ignites the garden with a burst of irresistible red flowers.*

PHASEOLUS COCCINEUS

fay-zee-OH-lus kok-SIN-ee-us

Scarlet runner bean

Scarlet runner bean (Phaseolus coccineus) **clambers quickly up a support for all-summer color.**

15'
1'

- Vigorous vine
- Perennial in warm-winter areas, annual elsewhere
- Fast cover for trellises and fences
- Short spikes of orange-red flowers
- Blooms summer
- All zones

Almost as fast as Jack's bean stalk, scarlet runner bean winds its way up poles and trellises and across arbors, creating a quick curtain of greenery that is soon decorated with spikes of red sweet-pea-like flowers. Simple and gratifying to grow, this vine is also ideal for large pots on the deck or sunny porch, where it can ramble up posts and along railings. Hummingbirds can't ignore the eye-catching flowers. Try it growing up a lamp post or a column.

CULTURE: Soak seeds overnight before planting for faster germination. Push individual seeds about ½ inch deep into soil in spring, after soil has warmed, at the base of a trellis or other support. When seedpods ripen, save some of the unusual speckled beans in a cool, dry place to plant next year.

RECOMMENDED SPECIES AND CULTIVARS: Plant breeders haven't put much effort into improving the species, which is excellent as is. The cultivar 'Dwarf' grows like a bush bean instead of a climber; try it as a patio edger. A white-flowered cultivar is available, but the red species is best for attracting hummingbirds.

PHLOX PANICULATA

floks puh-nih-kew-LAY-tuh

Garden phlox

36"

24"

- Long-lived perennial
- Clusters of blossoms in pink, purple, white, red
- 2 to 4 feet tall
- Blooms for weeks, summer into fall
- Zones 4 to 9

A trusted perennial from Grandma's garden, sweet-scented phlox attracts both hummingbirds and butterflies to its heads of small tubular blossoms. Many cultivars in various colors are available. The plants may self-sow and revert to the original pink and purple of the species, a native wildflower of the eastern half of the country that thrives at the shady edges of woods.

CULTURE: Plant the species in part to full shade; cultivars do best in full sun. Pinch the tips of each stem when about 18 inches high to encourage side branches and thus more flowers. Mildew may disfigure the foliage with a whitish cast; it usually does not affect the life of the plant, only its looks.

RECOMMENDED SPECIES AND CULTIVARS: Garden phlox cultivars and hybrids are easier to locate than the species. There are many excellent choices. 'Crimson Red' and 'Scarlet Red' are good colors to catch a hummingbird's attention; 'Starfire' is a first-rate red with deep burgundy foliage as well. 'Bright Eyes', an old reliable cultivar, has pale pink flowers with crimson centers ("eyes"). Similar to *P. paniculata*, the tall phlox species *P. carolina* and *P. maculata* and their cultivars also have great appeal to hummingbirds.

Garden phlox** (Phlox paniculata) **is a long-lived perennial of many colors; this cultivar is 'Sandra'.

SALVIA SPP.

SAL-vee-a

Salvia; sage

18"

10"

- Carefree annuals and perennials
- Fire-engine red, blue, white, pink, and purple
- Blooms summer through fall
- Zones 5 to 10, depending on species; annuals all zones

The popular bedding annual known as scarlet sage (*Salvia splendens*) is just one of more than 800 species—not to mention cultivars and hybrids—belonging to this genus. Scores of salvias are native to the Americas, especially to hot, dry regions of the West and southward into Mexico and Central America. Fill your garden with as many salvias as you can squeeze in, because these long-blooming plants are irresistible to hummingbirds. Salvias are especially valuable in fall, when migrating hummingbirds are on the move.

CULTURE: Species vary in their requirements; consult your local nursery or garden center. Most do well in full sun to part shade, in average to rich garden soil.

RECOMMENDED SPECIES AND CULTIVARS: Any salvia that will thrive in your garden is worth planting. For red flowers, try *Salvia splendens; S. coccinea;* the very late-blooming autumn sage, *S. greggii;* and the shrub-size, pineapple-scented sage, *S. rutilans.* For blues, consider mealy-cup sage, *S. farinacea,* and its popular cultivar 'Victoria', frequently grown as an annual; culinary sage (*S. officinalis*); and cultivars of the hybrid *S. × sylvestris,* including 'May Night' and 'East Friesland'.

Autumn sage** (Salvia greggii) **grabs the attention of migrating hummingbirds in fall.

Scarlet sage** (Salvia splendens), **left, is a foolproof annual;** Salvia coccinea **'Lady in Red', above, is equally easy to grow from seed.

ADDITIONAL HUMMINGBIRD PLANTS BY REGION

In addition to the plants featured in the preceding gallery section, many more beautiful garden flowers are excellent for hummingbirds. No matter what area of the country you garden in, you can fill your beds and containers with dozens of flowers tailored to a hummingbird's tastes. Choose your favorite annuals, perennials, vines, shrubs, and even trees, and your garden will be buzzing with hummingbirds through the seasons.

In the lists below you will find more highly recommended hummingbird plants for your region.

Fire pink (Silene virginica) *shines like a beacon in shady places.*

Red hot poker (Kniphofia *spp.),* *a trouble-free perennial, attracts a male Anna's Hummingbird.*

ANNUALS, TENDER PERENNIALS, AND TENDER BULBS FOR ALL REGIONS

Annual phlox (Phlox drummondii)
Australian fan flower
    (Scaevola spp.)
Begonia (Begonia spp.)
Bugloss (Echium spp.)
Canary creeper
    (Tropaeolum peregrinum)
Canna (Canna spp.)
Clarkia (Clarkia spp.)
Cypress vine (Ipomoea quamoclit)
Flowering tobacco (Nicotiana spp.)
Four-o-clock (Mirabilis spp.)
Garden balsam
    (Impatiens balsamina)
Geranium (Pelargonium spp.)
Gladiolus (Gladiolus spp.)
Impatiens (Impatiens walleriana)
Jewelweed (Impatiens capensis)
Lantana (Lantana montevidensis)
Larkspur (Consolida ambigua)
Nasturtium (Tropaeolum majus)
Parrot's beak (Lotus berthelottii)
Petunia (Petunia spp.)
Red morning glory
    (Ipomoea coccinea)
Scented geranium
    (Pelargonium spp.)
Snapdragon (Antirrhinum majus)
Spanish flag (Ipomoea lobata)

NORTHEAST AND MIDWEST

Abelia (Abelia spp.)
Bearberry (Arctostaphylos uva-ursi)
Beautybush (Kolkwitzia amabilis)
Butterfly weed (Asclepias tuberosa)
Cardinal flower (Lobelia cardinalis)
Carolina rhododendron
    (Rhododendron minus)
Currant (Ribes spp.)
Daylily (Hemerocallis spp.)
Fire pink (Silene virginica)
Flame azalea (Rhododendron
    calendulaceum)
Flowering quince
    (Chaenomeles spp.)
Foxglove (Digitalis spp.)
Great blue lobelia (Lobelia
    siphilitica)
Hibiscus (Hibiscus spp.)
Horsechestnut; buckeye
    (Aesculus spp.)
Indian pink (Spigelia marilandica)
Lousewort, wood betony
    (Pedicularis canadensis)
Pinxterbloom azalea
    (Rhododendron periclymenoides)
Red hot poker (Kniphofia spp.)
Rose campion (Lychnis coronaria)
Rose of Sharon (Hibiscus syriacus)
Veronica (Veronica spp.)
Weigela (Weigela spp.)
Yucca (Yucca spp.)

SOUTHEAST, INCLUDING FLORIDA

Abelia (Abelia spp.)
Beautybush (Kolkwitzia amabilis)
Bird of paradise bush
    (Caesalpina spp.)
Butterfly weed (Asclepias tuberosa)
Camellia (Camellia spp.)
Cape fuchsia (Phygelius capensis)
Chaste tree (Vitex agnus-castus)
Chilean glory flower
    (Eccremocarpus scaber)
Citrus (Citrus spp.)
Cross vine (Bignonia capreolata)
Fire pink (Silene virginica)
Flame azalea (Rhododendron
    calendulaceum)
Hibiscus (Hibiscus spp.)
Indian pink (Spigelia marilandica)
Jasmine (Jasminum spp.)
Lilac (Syringa spp.)
Lobelia (Lobelia spp.)
Mandevilla (Mandevilla spp.)
Peruvian Lily (Alstroemeria spp.)
Pineapple guava (Feijoa sellowiana)
Pinxterbloom azalea
    (Rhododendron periclymenoides)
Red hot poker (Kniphofia spp.)
Rose campion (Lychnis coronaria)
Rose of Sharon (Hibiscus syriacus)
Rosemary (Rosmarinus officinalis)
Veronica (Veronica spp.)
Weigela (Weigela spp.)

Ocotillo (Fouquieria splendens) is a favorite of the Black-chinned Hummingbird.

Crocosmia 'Lucifer' is one of the best perennials for mild climates.

Hibiscus rosa-sinensis, *sensitive to cold, is a rewarding patio plant in northern gardens.*

SOUTHWEST AND CALIFORNIA

Aloe (*Aloe* spp.)
Bird of paradise (*Strelitzia reginae*)
Bird of paradise bush
 (*Caesalpina* spp.)
Blood-red trumpet vine (*Distictis buccinatoria*)
Bottlebrush (*Callistemon* spp.)
Bouvardia (*Bouvardia* spp.)
Cape fuchsia (*Phygelius capensis*)
Cape honeysuckle (*Tecomaria capensis*)
Century plant (*Agave americana*)
Cestrum (*Cestrum* spp.)
Chilean glory flower
 (*Eccremocarpus scaber*)
Chuparosa (*Justicia californica*)
Cigar plant (*Cuphea ignea*)
Citrus (*Citrus* spp.)
Coral tree (*Erythrina* spp.)
Crocosmia (*Crocosmia* ×
 crocosmiiflora)
Desert willow (*Chilopsis linearis*)
Flame vine (*Pyrostegia venusta*)
Flowering maple (*Abutilon* spp.)
Ocotillo (*Fouquieria splendens*)
Palo verde (*Cercidium* spp.)
Powder-puff (*Calliandra* spp.)
Shrimp plant (*Justicia brandegeana*)
Tree tobacco (*Nicotiana glauca*)
Winter jasmine (*Jasminum nudiflorum*)

NORTHWEST

Abelia (*Abelia* spp.)
Beautybush (*Kolkwitzia amabilis*)
Camellia (*Camellia* spp.)
Cape fuchsia (*Phygelius capensis*)
Chaste tree (*Vitex agnus-castus*)
Currant (*Ribes* spp.)
Fire pink (*Silene virginica*)
Flame azalea (*Rhododendron calendulaceum*)
Foxglove (*Digitalis* spp.)
Hibiscus (*Hibiscus* spp.)
Lavender (*Lavandula* spp.)
Lobelia (*Lobelia* spp.)
Montbretia (*Crocosmia* ×
 crocosmiiflora)
Peruvian lily (*Alstroemeria* spp.)
Red buckeye (*Aesculus pavia*)
Red-flowering currant (*Ribes sanguineum*)
Red hot poker (*Kniphofia* spp.)
Rose campion (*Lychnis coronaria*)
Rose of Sharon (*Hibiscus syriacus*)
Rosebay rhododendron
 (*Rhododendron maximum*)
Rosemary (*Rosmarinus officinalis*)
Twinberry (*Lonicera involucrata*)
Veronica (*Veronica* spp.)
Weigela (*Weigela* spp.)
Western azalea (*Rhododendron occidentale*)
Winter jasmine (*Jasminum nudiflorum*)

COASTAL AREAS

Acacia (*Acacia* spp.)
Agave (*Agave* spp.)
Aloe (*Aloe* spp.)
Bearberry (*Arctostaphylos uva-ursi*)
Bottlebrush (*Callistemon* spp.)
Butterfly bush (*Buddleia* spp.)
Butterfly weed (*Asclepias tuberosa*)
California fuchsia (*Epilobium canum* ssp. *canum*)
Cape honeysuckle (*Tecomaria capensis*)
Chaste tree (*Vitex agnus-castus*)
Coral bells (*Heuchera sanguinea*)
Daylily (*Hemerocallis* spp.)
Flowering quince
 (*Chaenomeles* spp.)
Horsechestnut (*Aesculus* spp.)
Lantana (*Lantana* spp.)
Lavender (*Lavandula* spp.)
Montbretia (*Crocosmia* ×
 crocosmiiflora)
Pride of Madeira (*Echium candicans*)
Red hot poker (*Kniphofia* spp.)
Rose of Sharon (*Hibiscus syriacus*)
Rosemary (*Rosmarinus officinalis*)
Salvia (*Salvia* spp.)
Texas ranger (*Leucophyllum* spp.)
Yucca (*Yucca* spp.)

THE NATURE OF
BUTTERFLIES

The Monarch migrates thousands of miles each year to California and Mexico. At its winter grounds, millions of individuals cluster on eucalyptus, pine, and fir trees, clinging to one another's bodies like huge swags of drapery. For more on butterfly migration, see page 51.

A butterfly is beauty on the wing. The color and animation these charming insects offer is reason enough to invite them to the garden, but their life history, ecology, and behavior are equally fascinating. This chapter presents many facts about butterflies in the wild: the reasons for their beautiful coloration, the stages of their astonishing life cycle, the drama of reproduction, and the story behind other unique behaviors such as roosting, basking, hibernation, and migration. A butterfly-attracting garden is always full of life. It's even more fun to watch butterflies when you know whether the creatures are sparring, spying, or courting. Most important, understanding butterflies in the wild helps you discover the best ways to attract them to your garden.

The proboscis is a mouth part similar to a drinking straw that the butterfly uncoils to sip liquid nutrients. A Western Tiger Swallowtail, top, gains minerals from mud; the Orange Sulphur, left, probes deep to reach nectar.

DISTRIBUTION

More than 700 species of butterflies are found in North America. Although the majority seldom appear in gardens, whether or not a butterfly is likely to appear in yours depends in part on its range: the broad geographical area in which a species is found. A butterfly's range is limited by many factors including latitude, altitude, climate, and competition from other species. The most important factor is the presence of suitable habitat: the combination of plants, water, sunlight, and other things that a butterfly needs to survive.

Some butterflies have a naturally restricted range—the Mission Blue, for example, is found only on a single mountain in the San Francisco Bay Area. And some butterflies—many of which are classified as threatened or endangered—have declining ranges, largely due to the destruction of habitat.

Most of the butterflies that frequent gardens, however, have extensive ranges, and are well-adapted to a variety of habitats. Some of the most familiar and beloved butterflies—including the Black Swallowtail, Clouded Sulphur, Orange Sulphur, Cloudless Sulphur, American Copper, Great Spangled Fritillary, American Lady, Monarch, and Silver-spotted Skipper— are expanding their ranges due to the increase in disturbed habitats where the plants they prefer thrive.

Scientists classify butterfly habitats in many ways, from broad categories such as meadow, forest, or desert, to highly specific ones such as riverside willow thickets. Plants are an important component of butterfly habitat. The host plants of a butterfly species—the plants that the caterpillars of that species feed upon—are often highly specific. Caterpillars of the Pipevine Swallowtail, for example, feed only on plants in the genus *Aristolochia*. Adult butterflies can be quite choosy, too, about nectar flowers. Some species prefer certain fruits for nourishment; others eat the sap of particular trees.

Knowing the range, habitat preferences, and favorite plants of butterflies are the keys to attracting them to your garden. In the "Gallery of Butterflies" that begins on page 52, each butterfly description includes a range map and the preferred habitat, host plants, and nectar plants for that species.

BUTTERFLY SEASONS

As you get to know the butterflies in your garden, you'll learn when to expect your favorite visitors. The first appearance of the season tends to follow a predictable timetable, although geography, weather, and other factors may have an effect. Look for the butterflies below at the times shown in most areas except the Deep South, where butterflies often appear year-round.

Butterfly	Time of initial appearance
Mourning Cloak	February–April
Clouded Sulphur	March
Eastern Comma	March–April
Spring Azure	March–April
Zebra Swallowtail	March–April
Red Admiral	April–May
Lorquin's Admiral	April in California June in the Northwest
Black Swallowtail	April–May
Great Spangled Fritillary	May–June

BUTTERFLY APPEARANCE

STRATEGIES FOR SURVIVAL

In order to defend themselves against a host of enemies, including birds, mantids, spiders, and other predators, butterflies have developed protective characteristics. The lower surfaces of the wings of some butterflies are cryptic in appearance—that is, they resemble and blend in with the butterfly's natural surroundings—and the upper wing surfaces are boldly patterned. These butterflies avoid predators by first flashing the bright colors of their upper wing surfaces while they are in flight. Then when they land, only the cryptic lower surfaces are visible and the butterflies seem to disappear from view. The underwings of many anglewing species blend almost perfectly with the tree bark on which they perch, and the wings have uneven edges, suggesting the border of a dead leaf. The Common Buckeye has evolved spots on the wing tips which look like eyes, and which divert the attention of birds and protect the butterfly's vital parts from being eaten. The "tails" of swallowtails perform a similar function in that they trick birds into biting off this expendable portion. From time to time, you may see a swallowtail missing a portion of its tail or perhaps a Common Buckeye with a missing wing tip.

Some butterflies mimic the coloration of other species that are distasteful to predators because of substances in the host plants their larvac ingested. The orange-and-black Viceroy looks much like the distasteful, milkweed-feeding Monarch; the black and blue top sides of the Red-spotted Purple and the female Diana Fritillary resemble the unpalatable Pipevine Swallowtail.

Camouflage is so successful among the commas, left, and the similar Question Mark that they are almost invisible until they open their wings. Ragged wing edges add even more realism to the dead-leaf look.

Caterpillars, too, are adept at looking like something they're not. The Giant Swallowtail has evolved caterpillars that perfectly mimic unappealing bird droppings.

The beautiful butterflies that visit your yard exhibit a wealth of different appearances, life habits, and behaviors. All butterflies are insects, with six legs and a body divided into head, thorax (midsection), and abdomen (lower section). They have two antennae and a proboscis through which nectar and other sources of nourishment are ingested. Their compound eyes are highly sensitive to color, including the ultraviolet part of the spectrum that human eyes can't see. Chemical receptors on the antennae and the feet are used for detecting odors by touch.

The butterfly's most exquisite feature is its extraordinary wings. Butterflies have a pair of forewings and a pair of hind wings. Each wing has an upper (dorsal) and lower (ventral) surface, lined with veins. The coloration of the wings distinguishes each species.

COLOR AND PATTERN

From the yellow-and-black swallowtails to the tiny blues to the richly patterned species such as the eye-spotted Common Buckeye and the Painted Lady, butterflies show a range of hue and pattern that delights our eyes.

The color of butterfly wings may be due to pigment in the wing scales or to the refraction of light, which creates structural colors. Some structural colors are iridescent and change depending on the angle at which they are viewed, such as the upper surface of the blues and the lower silver spots of many fritillaries. The blacks, browns, and yellows of other butterflies are colors created by pigments.

Coloration helps males select a mate, because they can easily recognize females of the same species by their color. Color can vary seasonally and geographically, as with the black form of the female Eastern Tiger Swallowtail, which has evolved to mimic the bad-tasting Pipevine Swallowtail in areas where this butterfly is prevalent.

MALE OR FEMALE?

Male and female butterflies of many species are often similar, with only a few markings and subtle color differences separating the sexes. The female Monarch, for example, is darker than the male, with a smudged effect along the black veins of the wing. The male has a black dorsal hind wing spot.

Other butterfly species show distinct color variations between the sexes. For example, the male Cloudless Sulphur has plain yellow wings, whereas each of the female's forewings is marked with a distinct dark spot.

REPRODUCTION

You are sure to see some butterfly courtship rituals from time to time, regardless of which species visit your garden. Watch for butterflies of the same species courting, dancing in air or on the ground, and joined together in mating.

Most male butterflies use one of two strategies for finding a suitable mate: perching or patrolling. Some males, such as those of the American Lady and the Gray Hairstreak, perch on an open branch and wait for females to pass by; other males, such as those of the Tiger Swallowtail and the Spring Azure, actively patrol an area, searching for receptive females. When the male butterfly recognizes a female of his own species, he quickly pursues her to begin the rituals of courtship.

THE COURTSHIP DANCE

Some think butterfly dances may be acts of aggression, as males attempt to drive one another away, or they may be courtship dances that are a prelude to mating. There is perhaps nothing more delicate to watch in the butterfly world than a courting pair of sulphurs circling upward together into the sky. Male and female butterflies often do a nuptial "dance" on the ground as the male tries to entice the female to mate; and unreceptive females—including those that have already mated or are of the wrong species—will signal that they are unavailable by spreading their wings and raising their abdomen high into the air, thus making coupling impossible.

MATING

Butterflies mate by attaching themselves to each other by the tips of their abdomens. Mating can last from a number of minutes to several hours, and sometimes the pair can be seen flying around while coupled. Often the male carries the female, but not always. In most species, males mate numerous times during their lives. Some females mate only once, whereas others mate several times.

EGG-LAYING

After mating, the female immediately embarks on a search for the proper host plant on which to deposit her eggs. Oviposition—the depositing of eggs by the female on the host plant—usually occurs when the female lands on the host plant and curls her abdomen up onto a leaf, flower bud, or stem. Eggs are laid singly or in clusters on the underside of the host plant leaf. Some

BEAUTIFUL BUTTERFLY EGGS

Butterfly eggs are beautiful to behold, but first you have to find these tiny treasures. When you see a butterfly near a host plant, note the branch or leaf that it lingers at. After the butterfly departs, look closely, especially on the undersides of leaves, for dots of white, orange, yellow, pink, green, or brown eggs. Follow a female Cabbage White on her rounds and you may find a tiny egg on the underside of a broccoli leaf. If you live in the South where the Zebra breeds, examine a tendril of passionflower to find clustered eggs like those above.

Some butterflies, such as the Painted Lady, lay their eggs singly, whereas others, including the Pipevine Swallowtail, lay their eggs in clusters of up to a few hundred. An inexpensive hand lens, available in the reading-glasses section of discount stores and drugstores, is the perfect tool for admiring the beauty of butterfly eggs. Using magnification, you will be able to clearly see the interesting colors, shapes, and textures of the eggs, which may be round, oblong, domed, vase-shaped, smooth, or ribbed.

butterflies, such as certain fritillaries, lay their eggs among the vegetation near their caterpillars' favorite host plant (fritillary caterpillars eat violets).

Test your powers of observation by trying to locate eggs on host plants. Butterfly eggs vary considerably in size, from the relatively large ones of the Monarch, 1.2 mm long by 0.9 mm wide, to the tiny eggs of small skippers, which may be only 0.1 mm long by about 0.1 mm wide. Watch adult butterflies to find clues to possible locations for eggs.

A couple of male Giant Swallowtails do their best to catch the eye of a female nectaring at a zinnia. Competition can be fierce for a female's attention.

BUTTERFLY LIFE CYCLE

Caterpillar colors are as striking as those of butterflies. Stripes break up the shape of this Black Swallowtail larva so that it is less apparent among the stems of its fennel host plant. As a last resort, the caterpillar can shoot out a pair of strong-smelling orange horns to repel enemies.

The miraculous life cycle of a butterfly, from egg to caterpillar to chrysalis to winged adult, is a time of seemingly magical transformations. Plan your garden to meet their needs at various life stages, and you'll attract more butterflies.

EGG TO CATERPILLAR

Each butterfly begins life as an egg that is deposited on or near a specific host plant (the plant species preferred by the caterpillar for food). Although female butterflies usually lay their eggs on the underside of a host plant leaf, some butterflies (such as the Silver-spotted Skipper) lay their eggs on a plant next to the host plant.

The eggs of most species hatch in four to 10 days. A tiny caterpillar, or larva, emerges, and in many species, eats the egg covering. The larvae eat the host plant with vigor, shedding skins several times as they grow.

LOOK FOR THE HOLES

If you spot a leaf or leaves with holes or scalloped sections missing from along the edges, a caterpillar may have been—or still be—at work. Most caterpillars eat leaves from the outside edge in, clinging snugly to the nibbled edge with their well-camouflaged bodies as they dine, so that to the casual eye they look like part of the leaf. Leaf-eating beetles, on the other hand, often nibble holes in the middle of the leaves, although some beetles and other insects and slugs also chomp from the edges. Look for frass, or caterpillar droppings, on the lower foliage beneath chewed leaves. It looks like grains of ground pepper, which may be fine to coarse, depending on the size of the caterpillar that deposited it.

GARDEN-WORTHY HOST PLANTS

Tasty plants can be good-looking, too. The host plants below are attractive to certain species of egg-laying butterflies (or moths), but besides being caterpillar fodder, they also serve a solid function in the garden design. Keep in mind that if butterflies discover the bounty you've planted, the leaves may look a bit ragged for a few weeks. They'll soon recover.

Plant	Host to
Aster (*Aster* spp.)	Pearl Crescent
Butterfly weed (*Asclepias tuberosa*)	Monarch
California lilac (*Ceanothus* spp.)	California Hairstreak
Citrus (*Citrus* spp.)	Giant Swallowtail
Dill (*Anethum graveolens*)	Black Swallowtail, Anise Swallowtail
Dogwood (*Cornus* spp.)	Spring Azure
Fennel (*Foeniculum vulgare*)	Black Swallowtail, Anise Swallowtail
Hollyhock (*Alcea rosea*)	Painted Lady, some skippers, Gray Hairstreak
Mallow (*Malva* spp.)	Painted Lady, some skippers, Gray Hairstreak
Nasturtium (*Tropaeolum* spp.)	Cabbage White
Spicebush (*Lindera benzoin*)	Spicebush Swallowtail, Promethea Silkmoth
Violet (*Viola* spp.)	Great Spangled Fritillary

Caterpillars are as diverse as the butterflies they will become. Some are spiny and dark, others are smooth and brightly striped, some have fleshy antennae-like projections. Some are large (the Giant Swallowtail is 2⅜ inches), some are medium-size (the Common Buckeye is 1¼ inches), and some are small (the Spring Azure is ⅜ inch).

After three to four weeks of eating, the larvae of most species are ready for metamorphosis. (The larvae of some butterfly species, including the Great Spangled Fritillary, may spend the winter in that stage.)

CHRYSALIS TO ADULT

After shedding its skin for the last time, the caterpillar turns into a chrysalis, or pupa. This transformation begins as the caterpillar's skin splits and the larva wriggles so that the wafer-thin skin rolls off its body, revealing the pupa underneath. Pupae come in various shapes, colors, and sizes. Some hang upside down; others rest upright, held in place by a silken girdle that the caterpillar has made before turning into a chrysalis. Some pupae are brown and mottled, some are green, and some are white, orange, and black.

It usually takes one to two weeks for the pupa to develop into a butterfly. Some

Miracle in the making: (1) A Monarch larva rests before transforming to pupa (2). The chrysalis (3) is jeweled with gold dots. As hatching nears, wing color is visible (4). The brand-new Monarch (5) has limp wings, which expand and stiffen (6) before first flight. The early-spring and summer generations of the Monarch may live a few weeks, although the early-fall generation that migrates south will survive about six months before mating and heading north.

species, however, such as swallowtails, pass through winter as pupae. In spring, usually after the first rains, which nurture the host plants and nectar flowers that the butterflies will be using to survive, these pupae complete their development into adults.

The adult butterfly emerges from a chrysalis to look for sources of nourishment and a mate with which to reproduce and start the life cycle over again. Most butterflies live two to three weeks, although some live as long as 10 months or more. Others live for only a few days. For example, the Spring Azure may live for only four days, although the Mourning Cloak (which passes the winter as an adult) may live for as long as 10 to 11 months.

HOMEMADE BUTTERFLY FARM

A container, a caterpillar, and a handful of the leaves it eats are all you need to have a close-up view of the miracle of metamorphosis. The Black Swallowtail and Monarch are good subjects, because they eat common plants and mature in just a few weeks. Look for Black Swallowtail caterpillars on dill, fennel, Queen Anne's lace, parsley, or carrots in your garden, and search milkweeds for Monarch caterpillars. Then follow these steps:

1. When you see a caterpillar actively eating, snip the stem and put branch and larva into a container, such as a large jar or a cage.

2. Provide a slim, bare stick for the larva to attach its chrysalis to.

3. If you use a large jar, cover it with a screen or a piece of cheesecloth.

4. Replace foliage with fresh leaves from the same kind of plant as often as needed.

5. Check the larva frequently. When you see the caterpillar motionless instead of eating, it may be preparing to shed its skin for a larger one or become a chrysalis.

6. After the caterpillar pupates, remove the container's cover and the food. Add a second, taller stick that extends above the container.

7. After a week or so, check the chrysalis for signs of color changes as the butterfly within develops. If you're lucky, you'll be present when the new winged creature emerges.

8. After the butterfly hatches, it will crawl up the tall stick you provided to stretch its wings as they unfold and stiffen. This process generally takes a few hours.

9. When the butterfly's wings are hardened, carry it outside and release it onto a flower.

BUTTERFLY BEHAVIOR

A Little Wood-Satyr soaks up sun to warm its cold-blooded body for flight. In the morning or on cool days, butterflies often spread their wings and bask to soak up heat—a process that may take only a minute or two. Patches of sunlight in shady places often draw basking satyrs and other woodland species.

ACTIVITY LEVELS AND FLIGHT

Butterflies are cold-blooded, and as such they require warmth to stir them into activity. Usually butterflies will fly only when the temperature is at least 60 degrees F. In hot weather, butterflies will be active in your garden earlier in the morning than they are on cool days.

At night and on rainy days, or when the wind is brisk, butterflies remain in sheltered roosts to conserve energy. When the wind drops and the sun comes out, they will once again return to the garden.

The patterns of butterfly flight range from the slow, lilting flight of the Monarch to the erratic darting of a small blue. With practice, you can learn to identify many butterflies as much by their patterns of flight as by other characteristics. Becoming more familiar with habits such as these will bring you closer to the butterflies, and them to you.

BASKING

Resting in the sun with wings or body turned to receive the warmth is a common butterfly behavior that you are sure to observe in your garden. Because they are cold-blooded, butterflies need the warmth of the sun to heat their bodies to a temperature that can sustain the activities of flight and feeding.

Some butterflies, such as the Monarch and the American Lady, bask with their wings open and perpendicular to the sun's rays. Others, such as the Clouded Sulphur, the Cabbage White, and the Eastern Tailed-Blue, bask with their wings closed and their bodies aligned perpendicular to the sun.

Because basking butterflies are often still for minutes at a time, they offer excellent opportunities for observation and photography. The Common Buckeye, for instance, which spends a great deal of time basking in open, sandy areas, occasionally skipping from place to place, is a good subject for butterfly photographers.

ROOSTING

At night, butterflies need a place to roost where they will be hidden from predators and sheltered from the elements. They often choose the underside of a leaf or a well-camouflaged portion of a bush. The best way to see where the butterflies are roosting is to wait until the late afternoon and follow them to their roosting spot; this is a difficult, but not impossible, task. Butterflies also roost during cold, cloudy, or rainy weather. In general, they spend at least 14 hours each day roosting, from late afternoon or sunset until midmorning the following day.

LOVERS OR FIGHTERS?

Watch butterflies in your garden and you are bound to catch sight of an apparent sparring match, in which two or more butterflies flutter around each other. This behavior is likely to be more inspired by romance than by aggression; when a female is in the area, one or more males may flock around her. A dancing cluster of two or more butterflies is thus likely to be a sign of sexual behavior. A single butterfly that darts after passersby is more apt to be exhibiting territoriality. The Pearl Crescent, Common Buckeye, and Silver-spotted Skipper may take issue with a bird, dog, cat, or human.

MIGRATION AND EMIGRATION

Several species of butterflies fly long distances at certain times of the year. Some depart to escape winter cold, others to explore more northerly territories during the warmth of summer. Those that fly one-way, without returning, are not true migrating butterflies: They are emigrators. Butterflies that engage in one-way emigrations, taking advantage of the summer heat to expand their range northward, include the Cloudless Sulphur, Sleepy Orange, Variegated Fritillary, Gulf Fritillary, Common Buckeye, and American Snout. Cold northern winters later kill these ambitious colonists.

The Monarch is the only truly migratory butterfly. It escapes life-threatening cold by traveling as much as 2,000 miles from its summer range throughout North America to sites in central Mexico and on the California coast. Monarchs from the East and Midwest travel to a small region of fir forests in central Mexico for the winter; Monarchs in the West travel to pine and eucalyptus groves along the coast of California. They pass the winter clinging to tree branches in huge clusters.

A startling aspect of Monarchs' migration is that they have never been to the areas to which they migrate. Monarchs that travel south in fall have only just emerged from

HIBERNATION

Some butterflies, such as the Mourning Cloak and anglewings, spend winter as adults hibernating in crevices of tree trunks and walls. These butterflies emerge from the pupa in early summer or early fall. After flying around until late fall, they seek a sheltered spot, such as a hollow tree or a vacant shed, in which to pass the colder months of the year. If you have such species in your garden, you may see one of them flying out on a warm winter's day in search of food. Sap is a favorite food of these early risers, and the same warm days that bring the butterflies from their hiding places also signal the rise of sap in the trees, where it may drip from woodpecker and insect borings or other injuries.

their pupae. Likewise, the Monarchs that migrate to northern areas in spring are perhaps the second or third generation after those that overwintered farther south, mated in spring, then perished shortly thereafter along their journey north. It is a mystery how these butterflies know where to go.

Pay close attention to new and different butterflies in your garden, or unusual peaks in the numbers of familiar ones. Depending on the region in which you live, you may be seeing emigrating or migrating species of butterflies on the wing.

TAGGING A MONARCH

Butterfly wings are fragile, but they are strong enough to carry a tiny tag that helps scientists identify where the butterflies have been and where they are going. Many school groups as well as individuals help band Monarchs, netting the butterflies as they take nectar at flowers to capture them for the brief, harmless application of the tag. If you join an established program, you may be lucky enough to discover where the butterflies from your own backyard travel.

Every tagged Monarch that is recovered adds to the information compiled about these long-distance travelers. The data from tagging the butterflies is helpful in determining habitat protection efforts and other assistance for migrating Monarchs, as well as showing the routes and the astonishing distances these winged creatures travel on their periodic cross-country forays.

To find out more about tagging in your area, contact your local nature center or state park, or get in touch with the butterfly associations listed in the resources section on page 79. Tagging Monarchs is a satisfying project for young and old and a worthwhile contribution to science.

GALLERY OF BUTTERFLIES

This gallery includes 35 of the most beloved garden butterflies of North America. They are presented in their scientific order; for alphabetical listings, see the index. Each gallery entry includes photographs of both the adult and caterpillar, a range map, notes on habitat preferences and behavior, favorite host and nectar plants, and other ideas to attract each species. The size given is the width from wing tip to wing tip.

The butterflies included here are a representative selection of species with mostly wide ranges, and of various sizes, shapes, and colors. Arranged by family, the entries begin with swallowtails (family *Papilionidae*), which are large and have tail-like projections on their hind wings; then whites and sulphurs (*Pieridae*), which are small or medium-size and often white or yellow; gossamer-wing butterflies (*Lycaenidae*), mostly small butterflies, such as the coppers, hairstreaks, and blues; brush-footed butterflies (*Nymphalidae*), which comprise a wide range of species, including snouts, fritillaries, crescents, admirals, leafwings, emperors, satyrs, and the Monarch; and finally skippers (*Hesperiidae*), which are small or medium-size (with some larger members) and thick-bodied.

FAMILY: PAPILIONIDAE (SWALLOWTAILS)

BATTUS PHILENOR

Pipevine Swallowtail

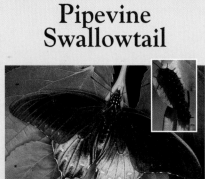

Pipevine Swallowtail (Battus philenor). *Adult basking, larva on California Dutchman's pipe.*

Found almost throughout the year in the South, and from spring to fall in the North. Ranges in open forests or fields where pipevine (*Aristolochia* spp.) grows, also in meadows, parks, and gardens, and on roadsides. Distasteful to predators because of substances the caterpillars consume from the host plant; coloration and flight mimicked by the Tiger, Black, and Spicebush Swallowtails, Red-spotted Purple, and the female Diana. Size: 2¾ to 4½ inches.

HABITS: Flutters wings quickly while taking nectar. Males patrol in search of females during the warm hours of the day.

HOST PLANT: Caterpillars feed on pipevine (*Aristolochia* spp.), which makes caterpillar and butterfly unappealing to predators. Use of pipevine in gardens is allowing this butterfly species to expand its breeding range. The caterpillar is black or brown with red tubercles (small, knobby projections) along each side of its back.

FAVORITE NECTAR PLANTS: Butterfly bush (*Buddleia davidii*), hyssop (*Agastache* spp.) lilac (*Syringa* spp.), azalea (*Rhododendron* spp.), and petunia (*Petunia* spp.).

PAPILIO POLYXENES

Black Swallowtail

Eastern Black Swallowtail (Papilio polyxenes). *Adult on* Cosmos bipinnatus, *caterpillar on celery.*

A common and delightful butterfly throughout its range. Found in many open spaces, including gardens, meadows, and roadsides. Frequent visitor to vegetable gardens in search of host plants of the carrot family. The Black Swallowtail is on the wing from spring to fall, longer in warm areas. Size: 2½ to 3½ inches.

HABITS: Lilting flight; flutters its wings when taking nectar. During cool periods, basks close to the ground with wings spread (dorsal basking). To deter predators, the female mimics the distasteful Pipevine Swallowtail in color, pattern and movement.

HOST PLANTS: Larvae feed on various members of the carrot family, including carrot, parsley, celery, dill, and Queen Anne's lace. Young caterpillars are black with white markings, resembling bird droppings. Mature larvae are green with black bands.

FAVORITE NECTAR PLANTS: Butterfly weed (*Asclepias tuberosa*), butterfly bush (*Buddleia davidii*), phlox (*Phlox* spp.), clover (*Trifolium* spp.), and thistle (*Cirsium* spp.).

PAPILIO ZELICAON

Anise Swallowtail

This species is found in a wide range of habitats, from mountain peaks to lowland valleys. In urban areas, it is often seen in vacant lots, canyons, parks, and gardens. Especially at home in California, where fennel abounds on roadsides, in vacant lots, in mountain canyons, and in gardens.

HABITS: Males spend their time on hilltops, where they perch and patrol in search of females. They occasionally "puddle" to take moisture from wet areas.

HOST PLANTS: Caterpillars feed on members of the carrot family, including carrot, parsley, fennel, and anise. Because fennel is easy to grow, this species can be raised from egg to adult indoors, then released. Young caterpillars are black with white marks, resembling bird droppings. Full-grown caterpillars are green with black bands and yellow spots.

FAVORITE NECTAR PLANTS: Lantana (*Lantana* spp.), zinnia (*Zinnia* spp.), butterfly bush (*Buddleia davidii*), and lily-of-the-Nile (*Agapanthus* spp.).

Anise Swallowtail (Papilio zelicaon). Adult on Verbena. Larva is displaying defensive odor spikes (osmeterium).

PAPILIO CRESPHONTES

Giant Swallowtail

One of the largest North American butterflies, this species frequents various open areas, including parks, gardens, and orchards. It is seen throughout the year in warmer areas and from spring to fall in cooler regions.

HABITS: A long, high, lilting flight pattern characterizes the Giant Swallowtail. As with other swallowtails, males patrol in search of receptive females. Males will also visit mud or sand, taking moisture from these wet areas.

HOST PLANTS: Various types of citrus trees, especially orange, are the principal host plants; prickly ash (*Zanthoxylum americanum*), hop-tree (*Ptelea trifoliata*), and rue (*Ruta graveolens*) are also eaten. Larvae (called orange dogs) are well-known as notorious pests on citrus crops. This notoriety is useful information for butterfly gardeners; simply plant a few orange trees to attract this lovely butterfly to the garden.

FAVORITE NECTAR PLANTS: Honeysuckle (*Lonicera* spp.), lantana (*Lantana* spp.), azalea (*Rhododendron* spp.), goldenrod (*Solidago* spp.), and orange (*Citrus sinensis*).

Giant Swallowtail (Papilio cresphontes). Caterpillar resembles bird droppings.

PAPILIO GLAUCUS

Eastern Tiger Swallowtail

This large swallowtail is found in woods, parks, and gardens from spring to fall and sometimes longer in warm areas. The closely related Western Tiger Swallowtail (*Papilio rutulus*) ranges throughout the western United States, feeding on some of the same types of flowers as its eastern relative and exhibiting many of the same habits.

HABITS: This high flier often takes nectar from flowering trees, but it will feed from shorter plants as well. Males patrol various areas in search of females. Like some other swallowtails, the female of this species has evolved a dark form that mimics the foul-tasting Pipevine Swallowtail.

LARVAL HOST AND LARVAE: A variety of trees and shrubs are hosts, including cherry (*Prunus* spp.) and tulip tree (*Liriodendron tulipifera*).

FAVORITE NECTAR PLANTS: Milkweed (*Asclepias* spp.), butterfly bush (*Buddleia davidii*), buttonbush (*Cephalanthus occidentalis*), Joe-Pye weed (*Eupatorium* spp.), and honeysuckle (*Lonicera* spp.).

Eastern Tiger Swallowtail (Papilio glaucus). Adult on statice, caterpillar on willow leaf.

PAPILIO TROILUS

Spicebush Swallowtail

Spicebush Swallowtail (Papilio troilus). *Adult on Mexican sunflower, caterpillar wrapped in Lindera leaf.*

Similar in appearance to the Pipevine Swallowtail, the female Black Swallowtail, and the dark form of the female Tiger Swallowtail, this species is mostly black above, with patches of metallic green or blue on the hind wing and white spots along the wing margins. It inhabits woods but also gardens, fields, and parks. It occurs from spring through early fall and can be found wherever its host plants grow. Size: 3 to 5 inches.

HABITS: A low flier, the Spicebush Swallowtail can often be seen on a somewhat rapid and direct flight pattern. Males patrol woodland and roadside areas looking for females and often gather at mud puddles.

HOST PLANTS: Larvae feed on spicebush (*Lindera benzoin*), sassafras (*Sassafras albidum*), and various bays (*Persea* spp.), including avocado (*Persea americana*) and red bay (*Persea borbonia*). Native to the East, spicebush and sassafras can easily be grown in home gardens throughout the butterfly's range.

FAVORITE NECTAR PLANTS: Honeysuckle (*Lonicera* spp.), lantana (*Lantana* spp.), azalea (*Rhododendron* spp.), and butterfly weed (*Asclepias tuberosa*).

FAMILY: PIERIDAE (WHITES AND SULPHURS)

PONTIA PROTODICE

Checkered White

Checkered White (Pontia protodice), adult and caterpillar.

This small butterfly inhabits usually dry, open areas, including agricultural land, vacant lots, and roadsides, as well as gardens. Often visits vegetable gardens to find larval host plants of mustard family, and visits flower beds for nectar plants. Found from spring to fall in cold-winter regions and year-round in warm areas. Size: 1½ to 2 inches.

HABITS: The Checkered White has a darting flight. Males patrol in search of females. Sometimes great numbers of this butterfly are seen together.

HOST PLANTS: Larvae feed on various members of the mustard family, including mustard, turnip, and cabbage. Spider flower (*Cleome* spp.) is also a caterpillar host.

FAVORITE NECTAR PLANTS: Aster (*Aster* spp.), butterfly weed (*Asclepias tuberosa*), centaury (*Centaurium* spp.), and members of the mustard family.

PIERIS RAPAE

Cabbage White

Cabbage White (Pieris rapae). *Adult on daisy, larva on flowering kale.*

The most widespread species in North America, this butterfly can be found in gardens, agricultural lands, vacant lots, and other open areas. A European import (formerly known as the European Cabbage Butterfly), it was introduced to Quebec in 1860. It has also been introduced to Hawaii and has become established there as well. Found year-round in warm areas, spring to fall farther north. Size: 1½ to 2 inches.

HABITS: Males patrol in search of females. They can often be seen mud-puddling in groups.

HOST PLANTS: Larvae feed on plants in the mustard family, including cabbage, cauliflower, broccoli, and radish, as well as nasturtium (*Tropaeolum majus*). They may become pests in vegetable gardens. Protect vegetable gardens with floating row covers to keep butterflies from laying eggs on the plants.

FAVORITE NECTAR PLANTS: A wide range of flowers, including lantana (*Lantana* spp.), impatiens (*Impatiens* spp.), marigold (*Tagetes* spp.), mint (*Mentha* spp.), and dandelion (*Taraxacum* spp.).

COLIAS PHILODICE

Clouded Sulphur

Males of this dainty, common species are fond of congregating around moist areas on roadsides and in gardens. The Clouded Sulphur can be found in open areas, including fields, meadows, roadsides, parks, and gardens. It flies from spring to late fall, and sometimes longer in warm areas. The closely related Orange Sulphur (*Colias eurytheme*) is more orange than yellow above. Size: 1⅓ to 2⅜ inches.

HABITS: Can often be seen basking with wings closed, sideways to the sun. Males patrol looking for females. The Clouded and Orange Sulphur may interbreed.

HOST PLANTS: This butterfly has followed the spread of agriculture; the larvae feed on plants of the pea family. Clover (*Trifolium* spp.) is a principal host for the Clouded Sulphur; the Orange Sulphur is partial to alfalfa. Although pests to farmers, both species are ideal for butterfly gardeners; clover and alfalfa are easy to grow in gardens.

FAVORITE NECTAR PLANTS: Aster (*Aster* spp.), goldenrod (*Solidago* spp.), phlox (*Phlox* spp.), and clover (*Trifolium* spp.).

Clouded Sulphur (Colias philodice) and caterpillar. Adult on Ageratum, posed to show open wings.

PHOEBIS SENNAE

Cloudless Sulphur

Found year-round in its range, in open, sunny areas, such as parks, gardens, and shorelines. Emigrates farther north during the summer; in fall, it often embarks on mass emigrations, usually in a southeasterly direction, because it cannot survive northern winters. Size: 2⅛ to 2¾ inches.

HABITS: Males patrol in search of females and often form mud-puddle congregations. Though usually a somewhat low flier, the Cloudless Sulphur will flutter up into trees to obtain nectar from the flowers it finds there.

HOST PLANT: This species' scientific name is derived from its host plant, senna (*Cassia* spp. *and Senna* spp.). Sennas are attractive plants for the garden, especially one in a natural style.

FAVORITE NECTAR PLANTS: Lantana (*Lantana* spp.), morning glory (*Ipomoea* spp.), bougainvillea (*Bougainvillea* spp.), and hibiscus (*Hibiscus* spp.).

Cloudless Sulphur (Phoebis sennae), adult. Larva is on Senna corymbosa.

EUREMA NICIPPE

Sleepy Orange

Common throughout its range, this striking butterfly is sometimes seen in large swarms on massive emigrations. It is found year-round in the southern states, spring to late fall farther north. It frequents open areas, including parks, gardens, vacant lots, fields, and roadsides. One of the "mud puddle" butterflies, it often congregates around puddles on roads, at shorelines, and in gardens. Size: 1⅜ to 1⅞ inches.

HABITS: Contrary to its name, this butterfly has a darting, erratic flight. Males patrol in search of females and often congregate at mud puddles. Usually seen singly in the North except during emigration flights, after which the individual butterflies become widely dispersed.

HOST PLANT: Larvae feed almost entirely on senna (*Cassia* spp.).

FAVORITE NECTAR PLANTS: Composites, such as tickseed (*Bidens* spp.), and other daisies. Also lantana (*Lantana* spp.).

Sleepy Orange (Eurema nicippe), adult and caterpillar.

FAMILY: LYCAENIDAE (GOSSAMER WINGS)

LYCAENA PHLAEAS
American Copper

**American Copper (Lycaena phlaeas).
Adult on Cosmos, larva on sorrel.**

This bright species is one of the smallest of the coppers. It is adapted to the disturbed habitats where its host plants grow (sorrel and dock, both common weeds from Europe), so it is commonly found in vacant lots, landfills, fields, and gardens. It flies from spring to fall. Adults vary in color and may differ slightly from one individual to the next or from one season to another. Size: ⅞ to 1¼ inches.
HABITS: Males perch on grasses or tall flowers and can be seen interacting with almost any passing insect. They may dart after or chase any trespasser.
HOST PLANTS: Caterpillars in the eastern range of this species feed on sheep sorrel (*Rumex acetosella*) and curly dock (*Rumex crispus*), sturdy perennial weeds often found in the garden. Western mountain populations select mountain sorrel (*Oxyria digyna*). Larvae are variable in color from rose-red to green.
FAVORITE NECTAR PLANTS: Butterfly weed (*Asclepias tuberosa*), goldenrod (*Solidago* spp.), yarrow (*Achillea* spp.), and buttercup (*Ranunculus* spp.).

SATYRIUM CALIFORNICA
California Hairstreak

California Hairstreak (Satyrium californica), adult and caterpillar.

This small butterfly with delicate "hairstreak tails" prefers dry, sunny areas, especially near oaks. It is found in open areas in foothills and canyons and in chaparral and pine areas in dry mountain regions. It appears from late spring to early summer, depending on elevation. It is similar in appearance to the Sylvan and Acadian Hairstreaks, two species whose ranges may overlap with that of the California Hairstreak. They are occasionally seen together, but usually the Sylvan and Acadian seek out moister habitats. Size: 1 to 1¼ inches.

HABITS: Often found feeding in clusters at wildflowers along roadsides or hillsides.

HOST PLANTS: Larvae eat the foliage of oak (*Quercus* spp.) and bitterbrush (*Purshia* spp.), both native plants in the range of this western species.

FAVORITE NECTAR PLANTS: Dogbane (*Apocynum* spp.) and milkweed (*Asclepias* spp.).

STRYMON MELINUS
Gray Hairstreak

Gray Hairstreak (Strymon melinus). Caterpillar in string bean.

This subtly beautiful species frequents a wide variety of habitats, including parks, gardens, vacant lots, and open fields. It is common from spring to fall. Because of its choice of host plants, it can be a pest to growers of cotton, hops, and beans. Size: ⅞ to 1¼ inches.
HABITS: Commonly seen perched on plants and rubbing its hind wings back and forth (as many hairstreaks do). Males often perch in the same spot on a shrub or tree for the afternoon, flying swiftly to and from this spot.
HOST PLANTS: Notable for the wide variety of host plants, which include scores of plants from more than 20 families. Corn (*Zea mays*), cotton (*Gossypium* spp.), hops (*Humulus* spp.), and beans (*Phaseolus* spp.) are some of its favored farm crop host plants. Others include hibiscus (*Hibiscus* spp.), clover (*Trifolium* spp.), mallow (*Malva* spp.), and vetch (*Vicia* spp.). Larvae range in color from reddish brown to green.
FAVORITE NECTAR PLANTS: Often seen nectaring on goldenrod (*Solidago* spp.), milkweed (*Asclepias* spp.), clover (*Trifolium* spp.), and winter cress (*Barbarea* spp.).

EVERES COMYNTAS

Eastern Tailed-Blue

This is one of the East's most widespread and abundant butterflies. From early spring through fall it frequents fields, roadsides, gardens, parks, and nearly any other sunny, open place where small-flowered plants are abundant. Look close to see the hairlike "tails" extending from its hind wings. The gray or brownish female looks very different from the iridescent blue male. In the West, the slightly larger Western Tailed-Blue replaces this species.

HABITS: Flies low to the ground, moving from one nectar plant to another. Spring females have bluer wings than females hatched later.

HOST PLANTS: Larvae eat the flowers and young seeds of many legumes, especially clover (*Trifolium* spp.), beans (*Phaseolus* spp.), bush clover (*Lespedeza* spp.), and sweet pea (*Lathyrus* spp.).

FAVORITE NECTAR PLANTS: A multitude of small-flowered nectar plants are readily visited, including clover (*Trifolium* spp.), zinnia (*Zinnia* spp.), lavender (*Lavandula* spp.), and goldenrod (*Solidago* spp.).

Eastern Tailed-Blue (Everes comyntas). Caterpillar on clover.

ICARICIA ICARIOIDES

Boisduval's Blue

This small, quick-flying butterfly frequents open or brushy areas. You may spot it in forest clearings, in sagebrush or chaparral, along coastal dune areas, or in fields and prairies, as well as in the garden. One of several species of small blue butterflies, Boisduval's Blue appears from midspring to summer, depending on the climate of the location. Several rare subspecies of this butterfly are indigenous to small localities. Among them is the endangered Mission Blue, a resident of San Bruno Mountain, a large wildlife refuge near San Francisco that is surrounded by cities on all sides.

HABITS: Males of this species patrol near lupines, the host plant, awaiting the arrival of females.

HOST PLANT: Larvae eat flowers and young seedpods as well as leaves of Lupine (*Lupinus* spp.), the host plant of this species.

FAVORITE NECTAR PLANTS: Visits many small nectar flowers, particularly those in the Daisy family. Wild buckwheat (*Eriogonum* spp.) is a nectar favorite.

Mission Blue (Icaricia icarioides missionensis). Caterpillar on lupine.

FAMILY NYMPHALIDAE: BRUSH-FOOTED BUTTERFLIES

LIBYTHEANA CARINENTA

American Snout

This unique butterfly, the only North American species of its subfamily, *Libytheinae*, is easy to identify from the extended "palpi" that project alongside the proboscis, forming a snout. It is resident at woods' edges, along streams and roadsides, and near hackberry, its host plant, but it also emigrates in mass flights when it can be seen anywhere, including gardens outside its normal resident range. The one-way emigration is in a northward direction. It is found all year in warm areas and from spring through fall elsewhere. Size: 1⅜ to 1⅞ inches.

HABITS: It can often be seen congregating at mud puddles.

HOST PLANT: Caterpillars eat leaves of hackberry (*Celtis* spp.).

FAVORITE NECTAR PLANTS: Flowers of shrubs and trees, including peach (*Prunus persica*), dogwood (*Cornus* spp.), and rabbit brush (*Chrysothamnus* spp.); many garden flowers including butterfly bush (*Buddleia davidii*) and zinnia (*Zinnia* spp.).

American Snout (Libytheana carinenta). Adult "stealing" nectar through slit in Lobelia cardinalis flower. Caterpillars on hackberry.

HELICONIUS CHARITHONIUS

Zebra

Zebra (Heliconius charithonius). Adult on Mexican flame vine, caterpillar on passionflower.

Distinctively shaped wings and color make the well-named Zebra easy to recognize. It frequents woods, thickets, forest edges, and raised islands of land ("hammocks") in grasslands and water, and is common in Everglades National Park. It is found year-round in the warm areas where it lives but may occasionally stray outside of its usual range, wandering into the Great Plains or the Southwest. Size: 3 to 3⅜ inches.

HABITS: Slow, weak flight, drifting from here to there; can fly fast and strong when alarmed. Individuals fly in to communal roosts at dusk to shelter together overnight.

HOST PLANT: Larvae feed exclusively on passionflower (*Passiflora* spp.). The larvae are white, with patches of brown or black in rows, holding black spines.

FAVORITE NECTAR PLANTS: Many flowers, including pentas (*Pentas* spp.), impatiens (*Impatiens* spp.), hyssop (*Agastache* spp.), verbena (*Verbena* spp.), and butterfly weed (*Asclepias tuberosa*).

SPEYERIA CYBELE

Great Spangled Fritillary

Great Spangled Fritillary (Speyeria cybele). Adult on swamp milkweed, caterpillar on violet.

Frequents moist areas, such as meadows, woods, and streamsides, and other open spaces, including gardens. In the West, it is often found in moist conifer or oak woods and openings in forests. The "spangles" that give this butterfly its name are silver spots on the undersides of its wings that glint like metal in sun. One of the larger fritillaries, it is found from late spring or early summer to fall. Size: 2⅛ to 3¾ inches.

HABITS: A fast flier, the Great Spangled Fritillary is a visitor of thistle and milkweed flowers. Males patrol in search of females. Unlike many other species, the Great Spangled Fritillary makes only one flight each year.

HOST PLANT: Larvae feed on violet (*Viola* spp.). The caterpillars are black with numerous black spines that have an orange base.

FAVORITE NECTAR PLANTS: In the wild, it frequently visits thistle (*Cirsium* spp.). In the garden, it is attracted to many flowers, including butterfly bush (*Buddleia davidii*), purple coneflower (*Echinacea purpurea*), gloriosa daisy (*Rudbeckia hirta*), verbena (*Verbena* spp.), and butterfly weed (*Asclepias tuberosa*).

PHYCIODES THAROS

Pearl Crescent

Pearl Crescent (Phyciodes tharos). Adult on New England aster, caterpillar on aster leaf.

This ubiquitous butterfly frequents open areas where its host plant, aster, occurs, including vacant lots, fields, roadsides, and meadows, as well as gardens. It is found from spring to fall in colder areas and year-round in regions with mild winters. Size: 1 to 1¼ inches.

HABITS: Males are active mud-puddlers and are often seen patrolling open areas in search of females. The Pearl Crescent basks mostly with its wings open. It tends to fly at lower levels.

HOST PLANT: Larvae feed on aster (*Aster* spp.).

FAVORITE NECTAR PLANTS: Any accessible nectar plant in the butterfly garden may attract this species. Some favorite plants include common oregano (*Origanum vulgare*), mint (*Mentha* spp.), butterfly weed (*Asclepias tuberosa*), butterfly bush (*Buddleia davidii*), and composites such as aster (*Aster* spp.), coneflower (*Echinacea* spp.), Mexican hat *Ratibida* spp.), and black-eyed Susan (*Rudbeckia* spp.).

POLYGONIA INTERROGATIONIS

Question Mark

When its jagged wings are closed, this butterfly looks like a bit of dead leaf. A tiny silver-white question mark, distinctive when wings are closed, gives this butterfly its interesting name. It is found from spring through fall in open spots near woods, along roads and streamsides, and in parks, orchards, and gardens. Wings have lovely lilac edging in fall and spring. Size: 2⅜ to 2⅝ inches.

HABITS: Not attracted by nectar, this butterfly prefers fruit, sap, and even carrion and manure. Often sips sap from bird or insect holes in trees; hard to see against the bark until the butterfly opens its wings with a flash of orange.

HOST PLANTS: Larvae eat leaves of elm (*Ulmus* spp.), as well as hops (*Humulus* spp.) and nettle (*Urtica* spp. and other members of the family *Urticaceae*).

FAVORITE FOODS: Easily drawn to overripe or rotting fruit. Plant pear, apple, and crabapple trees, and put out fruit feeders in garden.

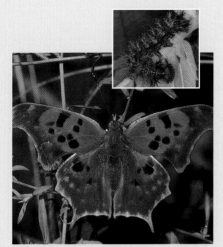

Question Mark (Polygonia interrogationis), *adult and larva.*

POLYGONIA COMMA

Eastern Comma

A common species easy to overlook due its excellent camouflage, this butterfly shows orange and black color when it opens its wings. Note the whitish comma inscribed on its hind wings. Found near woods' edges and clearings, streamsides, moist woods, and gardens, from early spring to fall. Rarely interested in nectar but eagerly comes to fallen crabapples or other fruit, as well as manure and carrion. Size: 1¾ to 2 inches.

HABITS: Feisty butterfly that often darts after people and animals, as well as other butterflies, insects, and hummingbirds. Often perches upside down on a tree, where it is nearly impossible to discern against the bark. Fond of sipping sap from trees. May sip sweat from a passerby's skin.

HOST PLANTS: Larvae eat leaves of elm (*Ulmus* spp.), hops (*Humulus* spp.), and nettle (*Urtica* spp.).

FAVORITE FOODS: Attract with an offering of overripe or rotting fruit, and plant fruit trees for future attraction. Particularly fond of pears and crabapples.

Eastern Comma (Polygonia comma), *adult and caterpillar.*

NYMPHALIS ANTIOPA

Mourning Cloak

One of the earliest butterflies to appear in spring, the Mourning Cloak may even be seen on warm winter days, when overwintering adults may venture out. It is found year-round at woods' edges and openings, parks, open woodlands, streamsides. Its beautiful coloring is easy to identify thanks to rich brown to maroon upper sides, edged with yellow changing to white with age, and a border of bright blue dots. It sometimes visits flowers but dines mostly on sap, ripe to rotting fruit, carrion, and manure. Size: 2⅞ to 3⅜ inches.

HABITS: Hard to see when perched against bark. Wings make a click when it snaps into flight that is audible from several feet away.

HOST PLANTS: Willow (*Salix* spp.), elm (*Ulmus* spp.), and cottonwood (*Populus* spp.) are caterpillar hosts. Caterpillars are black with black bristles and a row of red spots down the back.

FAVORITE FOODS: Easy to attract with fruit trees or fruit feeders offering overripe or soft fruits.

Sometimes visits flowers of willow (*Salix* spp.), plum and almond (*Prunus* spp.), California buckeye (*Aesculus californica*), and rabbit-brush (*Chrysothamnus* spp.).

Mourning Cloak (Nymphalis antiopa). *Adult basking on hackberry leaf, caterpillars feeding on willow.*

VANESSA ATALANTA

Red Admiral

Red Admiral (Vanessa atalanta), adult and larva.

Found almost anywhere, from forests and parks to roadsides, farms, and grasslands, the Red Admiral often becomes a charming garden friend, riding about on a person's arm, shoulder, or head. It can often be seen chasing other butterflies about the garden. The closed wings are dull mottled brown beneath, but when the butterfly opens them the flash of red is breathtaking. The Red Admiral is found year-round in the South and from spring through fall elsewhere. It is fond of nectar flowers and fruit, carrion, and manure. Size: 1¾ to 2¼ inches.

HABITS: Quick, apparently fearless butterfly. Chases butterflies and other passersby.

HOST PLANTS: Nettle (*Urtica* spp.) and other members of the nettle family (*Urticaeae*), including hops (*Humulus* spp.) and false nettle (*Boehmeria* spp.).

FAVORITE FOODS: Visits many nectar flowers, including purple coneflower (*Echinacea purpurea*), butterfly bush (*Buddleia davidii*), chaste tree (*Vitex agnus-castus*), hyssop (*Agastache* spp.), and tickseed (*Bidens* spp.). Easy to attract with a fruit feeder or by planting fruit trees.

VANESSA CARDUI

Painted Lady

Painted Lady (Vanessa cardui). Adult on African marigold, caterpillar spinning silk cover on artichoke.

The most widespread butterfly in the world, this species is also known as the Cosmopolitan because of its wandering habits. In spring, great numbers may emigrate north from Mexico. The American Lady (*V. virginiensis*) and West Coast Lady (*V. annabella*) are similar but do not emigrate in such large numbers. Found year-round in warm areas and from spring until late fall in northerly regions. Frequents a wide range of habitats, including gardens, parks, meadows, deserts, and vacant lots. Size: 2 to 2½ inches.

HABITS: Males usually perch, often on hilltops in the afternoon, and wait for females to venture by. Sometimes mass emigrations can be seen flying low to the ground.

HOST PLANTS: Larvae feed on a wide variety of host plants, but especially thistle (*Cirsium* spp.). They also feed on mallow (*Malva* spp.) and hollyhock (*Alcea rosea*).

FAVORITE NECTAR PLANTS: Many, including butterfly bush (*Buddleia davidii*), chaste tree (*Vitex agnus-castus*), aster (*Aster* spp.), cosmos (*Cosmos* spp.), and buttonbush (*Cephalanthus occidentalis*).

JUNONIA COENIA

Common Buckeye

Common Buckeye (Junonia coenia). Adult on goldenrod, caterpillar on toadflax.

Distinctive because of the large eyespots on both forewings and hind wings, this beautifully patterned species is found year-round in the South and from spring to fall in other areas. It frequents a wide variety of open spaces, including fields, trails, roadsides, and shorelines, as well as gardens. In summer, Buckeyes emigrate north, often in large numbers, especially on the eastern seaboard. Because the species cannot withstand northern winters, it is a resident only in the southern part of its range. Size: 1⅝ to 2½ inches.

HABITS: Fond of basking on bare ground, this butterfly will return again and again to the same spot. It has a rapid, darting flight. Males visit mud puddles for moisture.

HOST PLANTS: Favored larval hosts include plantain (*Plantago* spp.), a common lawn weed, as well as snapdragon (*Antirrhinum* spp.) and toadflax (*Linaria* spp.).

FAVORITE NECTAR PLANTS: Many, including aster (*Aster* spp.), hyssop (*Agastache* spp.), chaste tree (*Vitex agnus-castus*), butterfly bush (*Buddleia* spp.), coreopsis (*Coreopsis* spp.), knapweed (*Centaurea* spp.), and chicory (*Cichorium* spp.).

LIMENITIS ARTHEMIS

Red-spotted Purple

Frequents woods' edges and open woods, meadows, streamsides, roadsides, parks, and gardens. In the Southwest, it is found in canyons and watercourses. Flies midspring through summer. The red-orange spots that give this butterfly its name are on the undersides of the iridescent wings. Coloration mimics the Pipevine Swallowtail, which is distasteful to predators. The Red-spotted Purple only rarely visits flowers but is drawn to ripe and rotting fruit, sap, and honeydew produced by aphids, as well as to carrion and manure. Size: 3 to 3⅜ inches.

HABITS: Frequents mud puddles.

HOST PLANTS: Larval host plants include willow (*Salix* spp.), cherry (*Prunus* spp.), apple (*Malus* spp.), poplar and aspen (*Populus* spp.), hawthorn (*Crataegus* spp.), and hornbeam (*Carpinus* spp.).

FAVORITE FOODS: Plant pear, apple, and other fruit trees and supply a fruit feeder to bring Red-spotted Purples to your yard. Will rarely visit flowers of Viburnum (*Viburnum* spp.) and red-osier dogwood (*Cornus stolonifera*).

Red-spotted Purple (Limenitis arthemis). *Adult resting on leaf, caterpillar on blackberry leaf.*

LIMENITIS ARCHIPPUS

Viceroy

Frequents a wide variety of open spaces, including fields, marshes, roadsides, wood edges, and shorelines, as well as gardens. Found from spring through fall, but often there is a gap between flights when no Viceroys are present. Early in the season, the Viceroy dines on carrion, manure, and fungi. Later it seeks flowers. Northern Viceroys mimic the colors of the distasteful Monarch to deter predators; southern Viceroys are darker orange, mimicking the equally distasteful Queen. Curving black lines across the hind wing help distinguish the Viceroy from the Monarch. Size: 2⅝ to 3 inches.

HABITS: Bursts of rapid, flapping flight followed by a short glide.

HOST PLANTS: Favored larval host is willow (*Salix* spp.); poplar and aspen (*Populus* spp.) are also eaten. The humped larva is mottled brown to olive green, saddled with a brown patch on the back and a pair of bristles behind the head.

FAVORITE NECTAR PLANTS: Aster (*Aster* spp.), goldenrod (*Solidago* spp.), Joe-Pye weed (*Eupatorium* spp.), tickseed (*Bidens* spp.), and thistle (*Cirsium* spp.).

Viceroy (Limenitis archippus), *adult and caterpillar.*

LIMENITIS LORQUINI

Lorquin's Admiral

Lorquin's Admiral is the common admiral of the West Coast, and the smallest of the admirals. From spring to fall it is found anywhere in its range near larval host plants, generally near rivers and other watercourses, at the edges of woods, in parks, and in gardens. Its coloration mimics the California Sister (see page 62). Although the Lorquin's Admiral takes nectar at flowers, it also dines on tree sap, carrion, overripe fruit, and manure. Size: 2¼ to 2¾ inches.

HABITS: This aggressive butterfly zips out to challenge any moving creature, from insects to large birds and humans. Opens and closes wings to a 45 degree angle when basking. Flight pattern is flapping followed by a glide.

HOST PLANTS: Caterpillars dine on willow (*Salix* spp.), poplar (*Populus* spp.), and chokecherry (*Prunus virginiana*).

FAVORITE FOODS: Tree sap, carrion, overripe fruit, manure, and nectar from flowers of California buckeye (*Aesculus californica*), privet (*Ligustrum* spp.), yerba buena (*Micromeria* spp.), California lilac (*Ceanothus* spp.), and blackberry (*Rubus* spp.).

Lorquin's Admiral (Limenitis lorquini), *adult and caterpillar.*

ADELPHA BREDOWII
California Sister

California Sister (Adelpha bredowii), adult and caterpillar.

Some people think the markings of this large admiral are similar to a nun's habit, hence the common name, California Sister. It is found from spring to fall except in mountainous desert areas, where it occurs only during late spring to early summer. The California Sister frequents oak groves and also is found along the coast and on islands off California. It rarely sips nectar at flowers but is more apt to seek overripe, dropped fruit. It is often found taking moisture from damp mud and sand along the coast and rivers. Size: 2⅞ to 3⅜ inches.

HABITS: Frequents the upper branches of live oaks. May be seen at muddy areas or on moist sand.

HOST PLANT: Oak is the host plant for the California Sister. Larvae feed mainly on canyon live oak (*Quercus chrysolepis*) and coast live oak (*Q. agrifolia*).

FAVORITE FOODS: Offer a fruit feeder with overripe grapes and other soft fruits. A saucer of grape juice is also welcome. It rarely visits flowers but has been known to take nectar from the flowers of the California buckeye (*Aesculus californica*). A mud puddle may attract its attention.

ASTEROCAMPA CELTIS
Hackberry Emperor

Hackberry Emperor (Asterocampa celtis), adult and caterpillar.

A common butterfly wherever its host plant, hackberry, grows, this species is found in parks, farmland, cities, woodlands, and gardens. It is seen in summer in the North, but in more southerly parts of its range it flies from spring through fall. It is easily overlooked because of its coloration, which provides excellent camouflage against tree bark. The Hackberry Emperor is not attracted to flowers; it eats overripe fruit as well as tree sap, aphid honeydew, carrion, and manure. Size: 1¾ to 2¼ inches.

HABITS: Perches on tree leaves with wings widespread. May alight on skin to sip perspiration.

HOST PLANT: Hackberry (*Celtis* spp.) is the only food of the caterpillars, which are bright greenish, striped yellow, with a pair of tails at either end and a pair of horns on the head.

FAVORITE FOODS: Butterflies are attracted to overripe fruit. Plant fruit trees and provide a fruit feeder of pears, apples, dropped crabapples, melons, bananas, and other fruits.

MEGISTO CYMELA
Little Wood-Satyr

Little Wood-Satyr (Megisto cymela), adult and caterpillar.

One of many species of small brown butterflies called satyrs, this woodland inhabitant is actually bigger than most of its kind. The eyespots are typical of most satyrs. Found spring to fall, the Little Wood-Satyr frequents woods, thickets, meadows, and clearings. Unlike most butterflies, this species is attracted to a shady, woodland-type garden. Size: 1¾ to 1⅞ inches.

HABITS: Slow, erratic, dancing flight. May reproduce in great abundance.

HOST PLANTS: Plants in the grass family (*Gramineae*) are the food of the caterpillar; members of the sedge family (*Cyperaceae*) may also be host plants. Larva is brown or green, dotted with white tubercles.

FAVORITE FOODS: The Little Wood-Satyr sips tree sap, aphid honeydew, and manure. There are reports of it nectaring at hydrangea (*Hydrangea* spp.), privet (*Ligustrum* spp.), and peony (*Paeonia* spp.), although most authorities assert that this butterfly does not nectar at flowers at all.

DANAUS PLEXIPPUS

Monarch

The best-known American butterfly, found in open fields, meadows, and roadsides where milkweed abounds, as well as in parks and gardens in populated areas. In warm areas, it can be seen year-round; in colder regions, look for the Monarch from spring to fall. This is the only truly migratory butterfly; eastern and midwestern individuals overwinter in the fir forests of central Mexico, and far western individuals travel to the California coast for the winter. Size: 3½ to 4 inches.

HABITS: Soft, lilting flight. Overwintering congregations cover entire pines and eucalyptus in California (firs in Mexico), occasionally foraging for nectar or water, especially on warm days.

HOST PLANTS: Milkweed (*Asclepias* spp.) and other plants in the milkweed family, which add unpalatable chemicals to caterpillars and adults, protecting them from predation. The Viceroy has evolved coloring that mimics the Monarch and deters predators.

FAVORITE NECTAR PLANTS: Easily attracted to flowers. Many favored plants, including butterfly bush (*Buddelia davidii*), milkweed (*Asclepias* spp.), lantana (*Lantana* spp.), lilac (*Syringa*) spp., cosmos (*Cosmos* spp.), goldenrod (*Solidago* spp.), and zinnia (*Zinnia* spp.).

*Monarch (Danaus plexippus). **Adult nectaring on swamp milkweed, caterpillar feeding on butterfly weed.***

FAMILY HESPERIIDAE: SKIPPERS

EPARGYREUS CLARUS

Silver-spotted Skipper

Common in both city and country, this species frequents open and disturbed land, including gardens, parks, fields, and canyons. It is found from late spring to early summer in the North and West and almost all year in the far South. The silver patch on the hind wing is highly visible in flight. Size: 1¾ to 2½ inches.

HABITS: Like other skippers, the Silver-spotted has a fast, erratic flight pattern, "skipping" from one place to another. Males usually perch and wait for females to pass.

HOST PLANTS: Caterpillars feed primarily on locust (*Robinia* spp.). They also feed on numerous other legumes, including wisteria (*Wisteria* spp.) and beans (*Phaseolus* spp.).

FAVORITE NECTAR PLANTS: A multitude, including zinnia (*Zinnia* spp.), honeysuckle (*Lonicera* spp.), butterfly weed (*Asclepias tuberosa*), and Joe-Pye weed (*Eupatorium* spp.).

*Silver-spotted Skipper (Epargyreus clarus), **adult and caterpillar.***

PYRGUS COMMUNIS

Common Checkered-Skipper

A frequent garden visitor, the well-named Common Checkered-Skipper and its nearly identical western relative, the White Checkered-Skipper (*Pyrgus albescens*), can be found in a wide variety of open areas, such as gardens, parks, roadsides, and fields. Because of their small size, they are easy to overlook; take a close look at nectar flowers to spot these species. They are seen throughout the year in the Deep South and from spring to fall farther north. Size: ¾ to 1¼ inches.

HABITS: This is a fast flier that usually takes many short flights rather than long ones. Males patrol in search of females.

HOST PLANTS: Various members of the mallow family, including mallow (*Malva* spp.), and hollyhock (*Alcea rosea*), are usual host plants.

FAVORITE NECTAR PLANTS: Many, including aster (*Aster* spp.), butterfly bush (*Buddleia davidii*), fleabane (*Erigeron* spp.), knapweed (*Centaurea* spp.), rabbitbrush (*Chrysothamnus* spp.), and marigold (*Tagetes* spp.).

*Common Checkered-Skipper (Pyrgus communis), **adult and caterpillar.***

BUTTERFLIES
IN THE GARDEN

Purple coneflower (Echinacea purpurea) *and orange butterfly weed* (Asclepias tuberosa) *are superb nectar flowers for butterflies. Pearly everlasting* (Anaphalis margaritacea) *is a favorite caterpillar host plant for the American Lady.*

A Great Spangled Fritillary flashes like old gold when it opens its wings in a sunny garden, but it gets its name from the Latin for "dice cup," referring to its dotted markings.

ELEMENTS OF A BUTTERFLY-FRIENDLY GARDEN

A successful butterfly garden is one that provides the beauty of design and planting that appeals to the gardener while containing the following elements that butterflies need for food, shelter, and breeding:

■ Sunlight to keep their bodies working effectively

■ Sources of food for adult butterflies
■ Sources of food for caterpillars
■ A source of water
■ Hospitable surroundings that offer cover from the elements, provide a place to spend the night, and, in general, approximate the environment of their natural world

The best way to tempt butterflies to visit your garden is to provide them with nectar flowers. Nectar is a primary food source for most butterflies, which seek it from a variety of flowering annuals, perennials, shrubs, trees, vines, and herbs. Fortunately, the flowers that butterflies favor for food are often the same ones that gardeners choose for beauty.

BUTTERFLY FLOWERS

Butterflies prefer nectar plants that offer many flowers concentrated in one place for efficient feeding. They are attracted to tubular flowers, but the tubular flowers they seek are generally much smaller than those that attract hummingbirds. Unlike hummingbirds, butterflies can't hover in front of a flower while withdrawing nectar. They need to cling to the blossom while inserting their proboscis. Three types of flower structures best meet these needs:

■ Simple daisy-type flowers, such as purple coneflower and black-eyed Susan.
■ Clusters of many small flowers, such as aster and goldenrod.
■ Spikes of small flowers, such as lavender, salvia, and butterfly bush.

A daisy may look like one big flower, but it actually comprises many tiny, tubular, nectar-bearing flowers: those with petals, or "ray flowers," around the outside, and "disk flowers" in the center that have no petals. Similarly, plants with clustered flowers, such as goldenrod, milkweeds, and Joe-Pye weed, have flower heads made up of a myriad of small individual blossoms. Salvia, lavender, and other spiky flowers offer a stem of small blooms that the butterfly can visit one after another without flying to another location. A few large, single flowers, such as daylily and hibiscus, allow butterfly access.

An abundance of purple coneflowers, black-eyed Susans, and asters in an open setting is ideal for tempting big, flashy butterflies.

MORE IS BETTER

In general, the more abundant a nectar flower, the more likely butterflies will be to select it. To make the most of the butterfly-attracting capabilities of nectar flowers, it's best to plant them in patches, not individually. Massed nectar flowers provide a large area of color or a strong scent that will attract the butterflies. Also, the larger the number of nectar-brimming blossoms, the longer the butterflies will stay in your garden.

It's easy to incorporate nectar flowers into the garden in a way that pleases your eye and your butterflies, too. With so many excellent flowers to choose from, you can find plants that suit any style of garden design, from formal to casual to containers. Select plants that offer a long period of abundant bloom.

BUTTERFLY FLOWERS BY SHAPE

SIMPLE DAISY-TYPE FLOWERS
Black-eyed Susan (*Rudbeckia* spp.)
Coneflower (*Echinacea* spp.)
Coreopsis (*Coreopsis* spp.)
Cosmos (*Cosmos* spp.)
Mexican sunflower (*Tithonia rotundifolia*)
Silphium (*Silphium* spp.)
Sunflower (*Helianthus* spp.)
Tickseed (*Bidens* spp.)
Zinnia (*Zinnia* spp.)

SPIKES OF TUBULAR FLOWERS
Blazing star (*Liatris* spp.)
Butterfly bush (*Buddleia davidii*)
Ceanothus (*Ceanothus* spp.)
Lavender (*Lavandula* spp.)
Lilac (*Syringa* spp.)
Lobelia (*Lobelia* spp.)
Mint (*Mentha* spp.)
Oregano (*Origanum vulgare*)
Penstemon (*Penstemon* spp.)
Sage, salvia (*Salvia* spp.)

CLUSTERS OF SMALL FLOWERS
Aster (*Aster* spp.)
Butterfly weed (*Asclepias tuberosa*)
Goldenrod (*Solidago* spp.)
Heliotrope (*Heliotropium* spp.)
Joe-Pye weed (*Eupatorium purpureum*)
Lantana (*Lantana* spp.)
Milkweed (*Asclepias* spp.)
Sedum (*Sedum, Hylotelephium* spp.)
Verbena (*Verbena* spp.)

BUTTERFLY GARDEN DESIGN

Nectar flowers are the key to enticing butterflies to linger in your yard, so you will want to include as many areas of flowers as you can care for. Choose plants that offer a long period of bloom and a multitude of small blossoms to get the most benefit. Arrange the plantings to accommodate the feeding and flying habits of your butterfly guests. For nearly all butterflies, full sun is best, especially in spring and fall, when the sun's warmth is most welcome. Opening up sizable sunny clearings will make dense woodland gardens much more attractive to butterflies.

FLOWERS FOR SHELTER

Butterflies need a sheltered place to feed where they won't be buffeted about by strong winds. Use nectar plants or host plants to create windbreaks. Shrubs, trees, and trellised vines provide a windbreak and can also supply sought-after nectar.

Lilac or weigela grow into sturdy shrubs that protect the flower garden beside them. A wall or trellis covered with trumpet honeysuckle or passionflower will work as well. Plant cherry, pear, or plum trees on the boundaries, too. All of these plants will serve as windbreaks while also providing nectar and, in some cases, food for caterpillars.

FLIGHT PATHS

Open space and wide paths allow butterflies to sail through the garden unimpeded. Meadows, prairies, and other wide-open spaces are a good choice for a sunny hillside or a backyard and are particularly attractive

Tough and trouble-free, ironweed (Vernonia spp.) provides plentiful nectar in late summer to fall, when migrating Monarchs are passing through.

INSECTICIDES AND BUTTERFLIES DON'T MIX

A natural setting for butterflies is both attractive and essential to their well-being. Insecticides will kill butterflies in the garden as well as their eggs and caterpillars. Read the labels of any products you use: Even the organic pesticide called Bt *(Bacillus thuringiensis)* is toxic to caterpillars. If you apply Bt to a garden to kill pest insects, you will also kill any caterpillars on the plant, because they will ingest the leaves and become infected with the bacterium.

Insecticides can also be toxic to beneficial insects that control pests—and butterflies—naturally. Overlook the occasional insect outbreak, and you'll have many more butterflies. If you are concerned about larvae on edible crops, use floating row covers to protect them from egg-laying butterflies.

Tall flowers in back stair-stepped to short plants in front let butterflies easily reach them all. Clockwise from top: Mexican sunflower, 'Purple Dome' aster, purple coneflower, zinnias in mixed colors, heliotrope, and 'Cloth of Gold' goldenrod.

to larger butterflies such as swallowtails and the Monarch. In shady gardens, include paths that wind through shrubs and sunny openings so that woodland butterflies, such as the Spicebush Swallowtail, can fly through at will.

VARIED HEIGHT

Plantings of tall and shorter plants satisfy butterflies as well as our aesthetic eye.

Some butterfly species, such as the Tiger Swallowtail and Spring Azure, visit tall flowers; other species, such as the Little Yellow and the Least Skipper, stay close to the ground in their search for nectar. Keep shorter nectar plants in front or along paths, where they are easily accessible to the small butterflies that seek their food at lower levels.

Line a walk with fragrant lavender or a bright mix of impatiens for butterflies that seek low-growing flowers. A group of tall sunflowers or brilliant red-orange Mexican sunflowers will vary the vertical plane of the garden while also providing high-flying butterflies such as swallowtails a good nectar target within their flight path.

FRAGRANCE

Although butterflies use vision to locate flowers and only "smell" flowers with their feet and antennae after landing, many of the flowers attractive to butterflies are also highly fragrant to human noses. For example, butterfly bush, with its strong scent, is often covered with butterflies. Other nectar flowers that exude fragrance include lilac, lavender, heliotrope, sweet alyssum, and pinks.

FRAGRANT FLOWERS FOR BUTTERFLIES

Alternate-leaf butterfly bush (*Buddleia alternifolia*)
Aster (*Aster* spp.)
Butterfly bush (*Buddleia davidii*)
Chives (*Allium schoenoprasum*)
Clover (*Trifolium* spp.)
Daylily, fragrant cultivars (*Hemerocallis* spp.)
Heliotrope (*Heliotropium arborescens*)
Lavender (*Lavendula* spp.)
Lilac (*Syringa* spp.)
Milkweed (*Asclepias* spp.)
Mockorange (*Philadelphus* spp.)
Pinks (*Dianthus* spp.)
Sweet alyssum (*Lobularia maritima*)

Include early-flowering plants such as lilac in your garden to provide nectar for the Common Buckeye and other early-spring arrivals.

FLOWER SEASONS

Select annuals with long bloom seasons and perennials that bloom at different times to provide a continuous supply of nectar. In warm-winter areas, where many butterflies are on the wing throughout the year, provide nectar in winter with such flowers as lantana, verbena, and bougainvillaea. In cold areas you will need flowers in bloom from spring to fall.

In cold-winter regions, spring and early-summer bloomers such as pinks (*Dianthus* spp.), candytuft, grapeholly (*Mahonia* spp.), wallflower (*Erysimum cheiri*), and lilac will attract early-appearing butterflies. In the West, California lilac (*Ceanothus* spp.) and lupines are valuable additions for early bloom.

Midsummer is peak time for butterflies, and the choices for garden-worthy nectar flowers are legion. Prime candidates include purple coneflower, blazing star, pincushion flower (*Scabiosa* spp.), the milkweeds (*Asclepias* spp.), butterfly bush, lavender, and nearly all of the annuals attractive to butterflies. In the West, the native buckwheats (*Eriogonum* spp.), sages (*Salvia* spp.) and monkey flowers (*Mimulus* spp.) are indispensable.

Late summer and fall flowers are highly prized by butterflies. Be sure to include asters, goldenrod, Joe-Pye weed, ironweed, and summersweet in your garden. California fuchsia (*Epilobium* spp.) is an especially valuable late bloomer in the West.

BUTTERFLY PLANTS

Above: A mix of flowers at various levels accommodates the habits of many butterflies, from small species that forage low to high-flying swallowtails. A diversity of nectar sources also attracts hummingbirds.

ANNUALS

The flowers known as annuals sprout, bloom, set seed, and die within a single year. Some tender perennials are also considered annuals in cold-winter areas because they are killed when cold weather arrives. Annuals are ideal for butterfly gardens, because you can plant them to offer an instant source of nectar.

Annuals often have a long blooming season, providing color for months. Annuals also allow you to change the look of the flower beds from season to season and are ideal for flowerpots and hanging baskets.

BIENNIALS AND PERENNIALS

Biennials, such as wallflower (*Erysimum cheiri*), grow a rosette of leaves the first year, then bloom and usually die the following year. Perennials, such as aster and goldenrod, offer the ease of one-time planting for bloom year after year.

Perennials are an excellent foundation for a butterfly garden. Seek out native perennials in your area; they are likely to attract butterflies that are already familiar with their blooms. Explore the huge variety of native asters, for example. They can fill your butterfly garden with flowers from summer through fall, when butterfly populations are often at their peak, and when migrants are moving through.

A butterfly border in pink, gold, and blue. Clockwise from upper right: Joe-Pye weed, swamp milkweed, Russian sage, pink dahlias, and rose coreopsis. Gloriosa daisies and lanceleaf coreopsis in center rear.

TOP TEN BUTTERFLY ANNUALS

Ageratum (*Ageratum houstonianum*)
Cosmos (*Cosmos sulphureus, C. bipinnatus*)
Globe amaranth (*Gomphrena globosa*)
Impatiens (*Impatiens* spp.)
Marigold (*Tagetes* spp.)
Mexican sunflower (*Tithonia rotundifolia*)
Snow-on-the-mountain (*Euphorbia marginata*)
Sweet alyssum (*Lobularia maritima*)
Verbena (*Verbena* spp.)
Zinnia (*Zinnia* spp.)

TOP TEN BUTTERFLY PERENNIALS

Aster (*Aster* spp.)
Blazing star (*Liatris* spp.)
Buckwheat (*Eriogonum* spp.)
Ironweed (*Vernonia* spp.)
Joe-Pye weed (*Eupatorium* spp.)
Lantana (*Lantana* spp.)
Milkweed (*Asclepias* spp.)
Mint (*Mentha* spp.)
Pincushion flower (*Scabiosa* spp.)
Verbena (*Verbena* spp.)

For a low-maintenance butterfly garden, select shrubs that provide bountiful nectar in spring and summer, such as the chaste tree (rear), 'Black Knight' butterfly bush (midrange), and Russian sage and blue spirea (foreground) in this design. Group shrubs to concentrate the display and attract more attention. Hummingbirds may also visit this garden.

SHRUBS AND TREES

Woody-stemmed shrubs and trees, such as butterfly bush, can be nectar sources, serve as large design elements in the garden, and provide shelter or windbreaks. Fruiting shrubs and trees are excellent for attracting butterflies that dine on fruit rather than flowers, such as the Red-spotted Purple or Question Mark. Place fruit trees in an open site so that dropped fruit, which is most attractive to butterflies, is easily accessible.

Shrubs and trees also supply ideal perching sites for butterflies. Males awaiting a mate or basking butterflies will position themselves on a leaf in full view, and resting butterflies may perch on branches or tree trunks.

Existing trees may be valuable to butterflies even if they don't produce nectar. Oozing sap has prime appeal for many butterflies, including admirals, the Mourning Cloak, and the Eastern Comma and Question Mark.

VINES

Use vines in your butterfly garden to shelter beds of flowers from prevailing winds and to supply nectar for adult butterflies and food for larvae. Native honeysuckle (*Lonicera sempervirens* and others) attracts butterflies as well as hummingbirds to its tubular flowers.

(Avoid planting the rampantly invasive Japanese honeysuckle, *Lonicera japonica*.) Passionflower is a host plant for the Gulf Fritillary, the Zebra, and others. Pipevine is a host plant for the Pipevine Swallowtail; the increasing popularity of pipevine has helped to expand the range of this beautiful butterfly.

PLANTS FOR SMALL BUTTERFLY GARDENS

In small gardens and containers, select annuals and other plants that have a long bloom period. Here are some of the best.

Ageratum (*Ageratum* spp.)
Butterfly bush (*Buddleia davidii*)
Cosmos (*Cosmos* spp.)
French marigold (*Tagetes patula*)
Gazania (*Gazania* spp.)
Globe amaranth (*Gomphrena globosa*)
Heliotrope (*Heliotropium arborescens*)
Lantana (*Lantana* spp.)
Lavender (*Lavandula* spp.)
Snow-on-the-mountain (*Euphorbia marginata*)

TOP TEN BUTTERFLY VINES

Balloon vine (*Cardiospermum halicacabum*)
Bean (*Phaseolus* spp.)
Bougainvillaea (*Bougainvillaea* spp.)
Dutchman's pipe (*Aristolochia macrophylla*)
Honeysuckle, native species (*Lonicera* spp.)
Hops (*Humulus* spp.)
Passionflower (*Passiflora* spp.)
Perennial pea (*Lathyrus latifolius*)
Trailing lantana (*Lantana montevidensis*)
Wisteria (*Wisteria* spp.)

TOP TEN BUTTERFLY TREES AND SHRUBS

Butterfly bush (*Buddleia davidii*)
Buttonbush (*Cephalanthus occidentalis*)
Chaste tree (*Vitex agnus-castus*)
Citrus (*Citrus* spp.)
Crabapple (*Malus* spp.)
Glossy abelia (*Abelia* × *grandiflora*)
Lavender (*Lavandula* spp.)
Pear (*Pyrus* spp.)
Privet (*Ligustrum* spp.)
Weigela (*Weigela florida*)

SHELTER AND SUN

An overhanging leaf hides a vulnerable butterfly from the view of predators and protects its fragile wings from rain or wind. Here a Checkered White seeks temporary shelter beneath a green roof.

flights. Perennials and other plants with large leaves and branching growth are another favored place for butterflies to seek shelter.

Some butterflies will also perch and roost in overgrown areas and patches of tall grass. In one area of the garden, let the grass grow tall and the flowers grow naturally without trimming. An overgrown area will resemble the butterfly's natural habitat and provide more protection from the elements than a single flower border next to a lawn.

ROOSTING AND HIBERNATION SHELTERS

Butterflies need a safe place to sleep at night, where their wings will stay dry and they won't be exposed to wind or rain. Some hibernating butterflies are present during the winter in all parts of North America: The Mourning Cloak

Nectar flowers are only the first step to attracting butterflies to visit your yard. To encourage them to linger in your garden, you will also want to provide for their other needs, including shelter, water, mud, and other food sources for non-nectar sippers.

Butterflies require shelter from wind, rain, and other elements, as well as a place to roost at night. Butterflies that hibernate in your area also need a sanctuary in which to pass the winter months. Providing roosting places and shelter from the weather will go a long way toward keeping butterflies in the garden.

PLANTS FOR SHELTER

Foliage is not only useful as a windbreak, it also offers butterflies a protected spot to roost for the night or during inclement weather. Exposed bare branches also provide a perfect place from which to foray out on courtship

BUILD A BUTTERFLY LOG PILE

Wooden butterfly "houses," which you can buy or build to attract roosting butterflies, usually fail to draw in a single customer. An open structure of logs may not be as attractive as a tidy wooden house, but it is more appealing to the butterflies you seek, providing many inviting cavities in which they can perch, roost, or even hibernate. A log pile is similar to natural deadfalls of trees and branches in the wild, where butterflies also seek shelter. Bark on the logs provides crannies for butterflies to seek cover in, much as they do under loose bark in nature.

To build a log pile for butterflies, place the logs crosswise—log cabin style—to create as many open spaces within the pile as possible. Make the log pile about 3 to 5 feet high and the logs about 3 to 6 feet long, depending on the space you have available. Cover the top of the log pile to protect the butterflies from rain. By using thin logs, you can create more layers and therefore more cavities for the butterflies.

Select a shady site for your log pile, so that hibernating butterflies do not get too hot and possibly perish. Plant nectar flowers and host plants nearby to attract the butterflies to the area. Also, because the larvae of some species, such as the Tiger Swallowtail, leave their host plant to pass through the pupal stage, a log pile built near host plants will sometimes attract larvae away from the host plants when they are ready to pupate.

Openings among a pile of stacked logs provide inviting places for butterflies to seek shelter from the elements. A waterproof roof, camouflaged by a final layer of logs, keeps the interior dry.

THE VALUE OF ROCKS

Rocks are a valuable addition to any butterfly garden. They provide a place for butterflies, such as this Eastern Comma, to bask and perch, and they collect dew and rainwater that butterflies can sip while perched on a secure surface. A rocky area in a sunny, south-facing area of your garden, where the rocks will absorb warmth, will tempt butterflies to bask. Embed rocks partway into the soil for a natural look.

With the rocks in place, you are only one step away from a butterfly rock garden. Next, plant groundcover nectar flowers such as sweet alyssum or rockcress (*Arabis* spp.) among the rocks, and add low-growing host plants, such as nasturtium and clover, for larvae.

hibernates in many regions, the Question Mark and Eastern Comma in the East, and the Satyr Comma in the West. It seems sensible to believe that they would quickly adopt a snug wooden roosting box, but unfortunately that is not the case. The wooden boxes sold as "butterfly houses" or hibernation boxes seldom attract any shelter-seeking butterflies, which seem to prefer searching out their own natural lodging, such as beneath leaves, within shrubs and brush piles, or under the bark of trees. A log pile such as that described on page 70 is much more likely to tempt butterflies to stay overnight or longer.

SUNSHINE AND BASKING

Warm sunshine is an essential ingredient of any butterfly garden; without it, butterflies cannot fly and forage for nectar. Ideally, a butterfly garden should have a southern exposure so that it receives the maximum sunlight throughout the day. Provide ample open space in the garden, preferably in the center, so that the butterflies have adequate room to fly about and catch the rays of the sun. In large gardens, approximate the natural appearance of a forest glade or mountain meadow by leaving an open, sunny area among the shrubbery and trees.

Plant nectar flowers in areas of near-continuous sun. Butterflies are more likely to fly to flowers in the sun than to those in the shade. Most nectar flowers thrive in full sun, so setting them out in the sunniest areas of the garden will be best for the butterflies and for the plants. In addition, females often lay their eggs on host plants that are in the sun.

Butterflies seek out places where their cold-blooded bodies can soak up heat from the sun,

or sun-warmed surfaces. Many sites are used for basking, from foliage and flowers to walls and rocks. Butterflies will also use brick or concrete patios, wooden decks, or even gravel or dirt paths for basking. Place nectar flowers, such as verbena, and host plants near favored basking sites to invite more visitors.

SHADE GARDENING FOR BUTTERFLIES

An area of full sun is the best place to grow most nectar flowers for butterflies, but you can still have a satisfying butterfly garden in full or partial shade. Many host plants, including spicebush (*Lindera benzoin*) and violets, thrive in shade. For nectar, turn to native woodland plants for luring butterflies to your shady garden. Look for shade-tolerant flowers in the daisy family, such as native asters and perennial native sunflowers, both of which offer nectar and serve as host plants to various butterflies. Another shade plant for butterflies is false or ox-eye sunflower (*Heliopsis helianthoides scabra*), a sunny golden daisy that thrives even in full, dry shade. Many of the satyr butterflies reside in woodlands, and other species will visit for the attractions they find there.

NECTAR FLOWERS FOR SHADE
Astilbe (*Astilbe* spp.)
Bigleaf aster (*Aster macrophyllus*)
Boltonia (*Boltonia asteroides*)
Calico aster (*Aster lateriflorus*)
Cardinal flower (*Lobelia cardinalis*)
Daylily (*Hemerocallis* spp.)
Downy wood mint (*Blephilia ciliata*)
False sunflower (*Heliopsis helianthoides scabra*)
Grapeholly (*Mahonia* spp.)
Heart-leafed aster (*Aster cordifolius*)
Honeysuckle, native species (*Lonicera* spp.)
Impatiens (*Impatiens* spp.)
Joe-Pye weed (*Eupatorium purpureum*)
Phlox (*Phlox paniculata*)
Wreath goldenrod (*Solidago caesia*)
Zigzag goldenrod (*Solidago flexicaulis*)

WATER FOR BUTTERFLIES

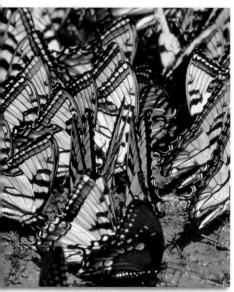

A puddle club of swallowtails (Eastern Tiger and Spicebush) partakes of moisture and minerals.

Boost your butterfly population by adding a water source for thirsty fliers. Many butterflies, including spectacular swallowtails and admirals, will be attracted to a simple, shallow puddle or even a sprinkling of water on paving. Mud puddles, where butterflies can absorb nutrients as well as liquid, are also popular.

MUD-PUDDLING

Swallowtails, sulphurs, blues, skippers, and other butterflies obtain moisture and essential nutrients and minerals from the moist areas around water. This practice is commonly known as mud-puddling. You can watch this behavior in nature by looking for butterflies at puddles on a sunny day on dirt roads or along the edges of lakes and at streamsides.

Mud-puddle clubs are usually composed of young, freshly emerged males that haven't started patroling for a mate. You can expect to see such mud-puddling butterflies as the Cabbage White, Spicebush Swallowtail, and Orange Sulphur just after the emergence of each new generation during the year.

Mud-puddling usually occurs during the warmest hours of the day, generally between 10 a.m. and 2 p.m. The butterflies, rather than landing directly on the puddle, will gather on the moist dirt or sand on the side of the puddle to obtain moisture without putting themselves in any danger.

WATER FEATURES

Butterflies may also be attracted to other wet areas in your yard. The moist soil beneath a faucet or around a garden pool is a good place to look for sulphurs and other moisture-loving butterflies. A natural or created stream or waterfall that has suitable perching places for butterflies to sit and drink may also draw them in. Even large rocks with irregular surfaces that collect dew or water from a garden sprinkler make a good water feature for butterflies.

Water is a desirable addition to the garden for people pleasure as well as for butterflies, birds, and other creatures. If you add rocks that allow butterflies to sip shallow water from a place of safe footing, your water garden will

SWEAT SIPPERS

Human perspiration may seem far from nectar, but several types of butterflies seek out sweat. The tiny drops of liquid are full of salt, a necessity for butterflies. Being the host of a live butterfly is an unusual experience. If you are working up a sweat in the garden and a Red Admiral, Hackberry Emperor, or other species alights on your bare arm, hold still and watch closely. You may see and feel the butterfly begin to tap its proboscis against your skin with a delicate, tickling touch as it sips your sweat.

PUDDLE BUTTERFLIES

- Most swallowtails
- Most whites and sulphurs
- Most blues
- A few of the true brush-foots, including the Question Mark, Eastern Comma, checkerspots, and crescents
- Many admirals
- A few satyrs, such as the Disa Alpine
- Many skippers

MAKING MUD

To make a puddle, remove the vegetation from an area about 2 to 3 feet across in full sun surrounded by open space. Scoop out a shallow depression with a hoe. Mix in a generous amount of sand and lay pebbles or gravel on top. The final depression should be about 2 inches deep in the center, with gradually sloping sides. Allow water to run slowly from a hose until the soil is saturated and the water pools on top. Keep the mud wet.

Choose an open, sunny area for a butterfly-attracting mud puddle. Keep at least one side clear of vegetation for easy approach.

Water is an excellent way to attract the Mourning Cloak to your yard. Many butterflies that eat fruit, tree sap, and even more unusual foods will readily come to a source of water.

soon attract a variety of species. Water is an especially good attractant during times of drought or hot weather, when more butterflies will seek it out.

Streams and ponds, either natural or artificial, are distinct assets to a butterfly garden because they are both attractive and practical. But even the minimal effort of keeping a bare path of soil wet will attract more butterflies to your yard.

Start a mud-puddle club of the Tiger Swallowtail or Clouded Sulphur by allowing a damp area or shallow puddle to form in the garden or by deliberately creating a puddle. Add a light sprinkling of salt to the water from time to time to provide mud-puddling butterflies with the sodium they need.

CLAY SAUCER DRINKING STATION

Shallow water and secure footing are keys to a successful butterfly drinking station. Although many butterflies will visit a source of water, they are protective of their wings and want to keep them dry.

Making a drinking station is fast and easy. Fill a shallow terra-cotta (or plastic) saucer, the kind sold for putting beneath a flowerpot, with smooth river rocks or other attractive stones. Place it at ground level or, for more visual appeal, raise it slightly on a layer of stacked bricks. Add fresh, cold water and refill each day. The water should be visible between the rocks, with some rocks partly covered or covered with shallow water and with plenty of landing places above the water.

SPRAY YOUR PAVING

Your sidewalk, driveway, or patio can be a powerful attractant for several species of butterflies. After you see butterflies on the wing on a bright, sunny day, get out the hose and thoroughly spray a patch of paving. The shallow film of water over brick or concrete is the perfect depth for butterflies, which are adept at siphoning up even small drops of water. Spray your paving every day and you may be honored with regular visits.

Incorporating water for butterflie[s] ... with small stone landing pads. 2. Midway along the walk is a large, concave ston[e] ... to it is an area of open soil with a mud puddle. 4. The brick paving is hosed dow[n] ... purple coneflower, 'Autumn Joy' sedum, and butterfly bush to the rear, orega[no] ... [a]nd geraniums in pots.

BUTTERFLY FEEDING STATIONS

The Red-spotted Purple prefers to dine on fruit. Offer ripe or overripe apple, peach, pear, plum, fig, banana, pineapple, and other fruit to attract such butterflies.

A garden filled with nectar flowers will provide food for the nutrient needs of many butterflies that come to your yard, but some species can be attracted by offering other kinds of foods. Sugar-water nectar, which you can offer in a special feeder, is popular with some butterflies, including those that normally do not seek out flowers, such as the Red-spotted Purple and Question Mark. Fruit feeders and a homemade "sugaring" brew that you can paint onto an outdoor surface will also attract many beautiful fruit-eating butterflies.

Adding feeders allows you to observe butterflies up close, while they are intent on eating. Feeders are good places to practice using close-focus binoculars or a camera to record your butterfly visitors.

NECTAR FEEDERS

A solution of sugar water is likely to attract butterflies to a dish or other feeding device, but butterfly nectar feeders have some drawbacks. Because the liquid is exposed rather than held in a reservoir as with hummingbird feeders, it will attract many wasps, ants, and other insects as well as butterflies. Commercial feeders, including the popular plastic daisy design, attempt to circumvent this problem by using a plastic screen above the nectar and a moat to keep ants from the liquid. Unfortunately, small butterflies, such as the Hackberry Emperor, may become trapped in the moat and suffer damaged wings as they struggle to free themselves. Examine a commercial feeder carefully before you offer it to butterflies to make sure it is not a potential death trap.

A simple saucer avoids this problem, although it will attract other insects and will need frequent cleaning. Boil 1 part sugar and 4 parts water until the sugar is dissolved, and allow the solution to cool. You can pour it directly into the saucer or line the saucer with an absorbent material such as facial tissue and saturate the material with the sugar solution.

UNUSUAL FOODS

Favored menu items of some butterflies, including the Red-spotted Purple, Hackberry Emperor, Question Mark, and others, are odd at best and disgusting at worst. Of course, that's seen through our human perspective. To a butterfly, nutrients are nutrients, no matter where they come from. Carrion is one of the favorite meals of several butterfly species, which congregate on a carcass to drink the strong-smelling juices. Manure from just about any animal is also treasured. Even fresh, juicy bird droppings are appreciated by some butterflies. Sap is another favorite. When wood-boring beetles or other problems cause a tree to weep sap, butterflies often gather on the bark to indulge in a snack. A top treat for many butterflies, including some nectar drinkers, is rotten fruit—a good reason to put your overripe peaches, apples, and other offerings in the garden.

ANTI-PEST MEASURES

Sweet stuff appeals to ants, wasps, bees, and other insects as well as butterflies. It can be fascinating to watch these insects as they dine, but if you want to discourage them, you can use barriers or greasy substances to keep them from reaching the nectar. To protect butterfly feeders from flying pests, cover the dish with a piece of stiff window screen, cut to size. The proboscis of many butterflies will be able to reach the liquid below, but shorter-tongued pests may be deterred. To discourage ant traffic at the feeder, place sticky tape on the post below the feeder or smear the post with a liberal coating of petroleum jelly.

Place the feeder near nectar flowers on a flat-topped post 4 to 6 inches higher than the tallest flowers. The flowers will attract butterflies and the feeder will draw butterflies to the alternative food source.

FRUIT FOR BUTTERFLIES

Some butterflies—the Hackberry Emperor, Mourning Cloak, Question Mark, and Red-spotted Purple among them—feed primarily on rotting fruit, tree sap, and even dung and carrion, gaining moisture and nutrients from all these substances. Many of these butterflies live in forest environments, where there are relatively few flowers that provide nectar. Over the course of their evolution, these butterflies have adapted to making use of alternative sources of nourishment.

An offering of fruit is an easy way to attract these butterflies to your yard. Fruit-bearing trees and shrubs, and feeders stocked with ripe to rotting fruit, will bring them in to feed on their items of choice.

BEST FRUITS

Nearly all fruits are eaten by butterflies. Experiment until you find those that appeal most to the butterflies in your area. Pear, apple, peach, banana, and pineapple are widely welcomed. Fig, persimmon, and crabapple are also appreciated. Cantaloupe, watermelon, honeydew, and other melons are favored by the Monarch and other butterflies. Even tomato is sought out by some species,

including the beautiful lilac-edged Question Mark.

Butterflies usually wait until fruit is overripe before they dine upon it. When fruit rots, the skin softens, making it easier for a butterfly to pierce to reach the juices within. Fermenting fruit is also highly popular.

SPECIAL RECIPE

A mix of fruit and strong-smelling ingredients is an excellent way to bring butterflies into your garden. Add stale beer, brown sugar or molasses, and yeast to a bucket of rotting bananas, plums, pears, or other fruit. Allow the mixture to ferment. Then pour some of the juice onto a plate feeder. The mixture gives off a strong odor that will attract butterflies. You can even paint it on the trunks of trees to simulate tree sap.

FRUIT TREES

Fruit trees and flowering crabapples make handsome additions to the garden. The fruit they bear will attract butterflies, especially after it ripens and falls. Because butterflies do not need perfect fruit, you won't have to concern yourself with potentially harmful sprays to get a good crop of butterflies. Choose an open site for fruiting plants so butterflies will have easy access to the fruit that drops under the tree or shrub. Apple, crabapple, cherry, pear, peach, plum, persimmon, and fig are excellent choices for planting to attract butterflies.

FRUIT FEEDER

A post topped with a flat piece of board that will support a plate of fruit is quick and easy to set in place, and it will draw in fruit-eating butterflies such as the Eastern Comma, Hackberry Emperor, Red-spotted Purple, and others. Install a flat-topped post so that the top is at a height of about 4 feet, convenient for observation. Nail a 12-inch-square section of plywood or a foot-long piece of wide board to the top of the post. Then simply set a plate of ripe fruit on the board. Within days, the fruit will soften, begin to rot, and become appealing to many butterflies (as well as wasps and other insects, which are also interesting to observe). Replace the fruit as needed.

CATERPILLAR HOST PLANTS

The fearsome larva of the Gulf Fritillary, a vivid orange butterfly, eats a diet of passionflower foliage (Passiflora spp.). Butterfly names that include a plant reference are clues to the menu of their caterpillars: The larvae of the Pipevine Swallowtail, Spicebush Swallowtail, and Cabbage White all devour their namesake plants.

Caterpillar gardens can be attractive to people, too. Between a background of Dutchman's pipe and a facing of parsley, this garden blooms with hollyhocks, false sunflower, borage, common mallow, tall pink snapdragons, and pearly everlasting. Bronze fennel adds soft, feathery texture.

Encourage butterflies to stay from generation to generation by providing the proper host plants. A suitable plant on which to lay eggs is just as attractive to butterflies as nectar flowers, and the larvae that hatch in your yard will soon take their place at flowers or feeders. You can plant host plants anywhere in your garden.

Butterflies often have narrowly specific needs for plants on which their caterpillars will feed. Various carrot family members, such as Queen Anne's lace and parsley, will attract the Black Swallowtail; in the West the Anise Swallowtail will flit into your yard for a generous planting of fennel. The Gray

Hairstreak uses many types of host plants, such as clover, hibiscus, and mallow. The Gulf Fritillary chooses only passionflower, and the Great Spangled Fritillary limits its larval feeding to violets.

Host-plant vines, such as passionflower and pipevine, make excellent wall, fence, and trellis coverings; host trees such as tulip tree (*Liriodendron tulipifera*, a favorite of the Tiger Swallowtail) can serve as an effective windbreak and shelter when planted in rows.

The white flowers of pearly everlasting and the delicate, feathery foliage of fennel add beauty as well as attract egg-laying butterflies; thistle (*Cirsium* spp.) and milkweed (*Asclepias* spp.) yield popular nectar flowers as well as attract the female Painted Lady and Monarch, respectively, to lay eggs.

PROTECTING PLANTS FROM CATERPILLARS

To protect certain host plant vegetables and herbs, such as cabbage, parsley, dill, and alfalfa, from being eaten by the larvae of butterflies, put netting or floating row covers over one area of the crop and leave another area exposed for the butterflies to use. The covering will prevent the females from laying their eggs on the particular host plants that you want to protect.

MOTH GARDENS

A garden that attracts butterflies will also bring you the nighttime bonus of moths. In the evenings and at night, big, hummingbird-like sphinx moths, for example, will sip nectar from many of the same flowers that attract butterflies and hummingbirds. Night-blooming, pale-colored flowers, such as moonflower and evening primrose, are particularly attractive to moths.

Thousands of species of moths roam North America. Many are dressed in subtle colors, but some are just as vivid and beautiful as the brightest butterfly, and several species boast a wingspan that can reach 6 inches.

A surprising number of moths do not feed as adults; they live for only a short span of days, during which they find a mate and reproduce. But even these species, which include the huge and beautiful Cecropia, Polyphemus, and other giant silkmoths, will visit your garden in order to seek host plants. Many of the same trees, shrubs, and herbaceous plants that attract egg-laying butterflies may also attract adult moths that are looking for a suitable nursery. The fabulous pale green Luna, for example, which flutters delicate tails from its jade green hind wings, seeks out various broad-leaved trees, including oak, walnut, and willow.

A few species of moths fly during daytime hours, including the Hummingbird Clearwing (*Hemarius thysbe*) and the White-lined Sphinx (*Hyles lineata*). Both look much like small hummingbirds as they hover before a flower. The Hummingbird Clearwing has a greenish body, and its wings soon lose their colored scales to reveal transparent areas that blur like a hummingbird when in motion. Hummingbird-attracting flowers, such as salvia and petunia, also lure this moth to a garden.

The striking underwing moths, which conceal bright-colored hind wings under their drab forewings, may visit your garden for overripe or rotten fruit at trees or in a feeder. You can also attract these and other moths by smearing a concoction of brown sugar, stale beer, and mashed overripe banana on a stump, tree trunk, or other surface.

Learning to appreciate your nighttime visitors will bring you additional hours of enjoyment in your garden. A bright outside light will lure many garden moths to a place where you can easily observe them.

The lovely Luna moth, its pale wings camouflaged by a tracery of budding twigs, is as beautiful as any butterfly. The day-flying Hummingbird Clearwing (inset) is a moth that hovers at flowers like a hummingbird.

Moonflowers on a trellis, white petunias in pots, and four-o-clocks, evening primrose, and heliotrope provide luscious garden fragrance and attract nighttime nectar seekers.

MOTH-ATTRACTING PLANTS

NECTAR
Cleome (*Cleome* spp.)
Evening primrose (*Oenothera* spp.)
Flowering tobacco (*Nicotiana* spp.)
Honeysuckle (*Lonicera* spp.)
Impatiens (*Impatiens* spp.)
Moonflower (*Ipomoea alba*)
Petunia (*Petunia* spp.)
Sweet alyssum (*Lobularia maritima*)

HOST PLANTS
Acacia (*Acacia* spp.)
Ceanothus (*Ceanothus* spp.)
Hickory (*Carya* spp.)
Maple (*Acer* spp.)
Milkweed (*Asclepias* spp.)
Oak (*Quercus* spp.)
Spicebush (*Lindera benzoin*)
Willow (*Salix* spp.)

THE BUTTERFLY-FRIENDLY YARD

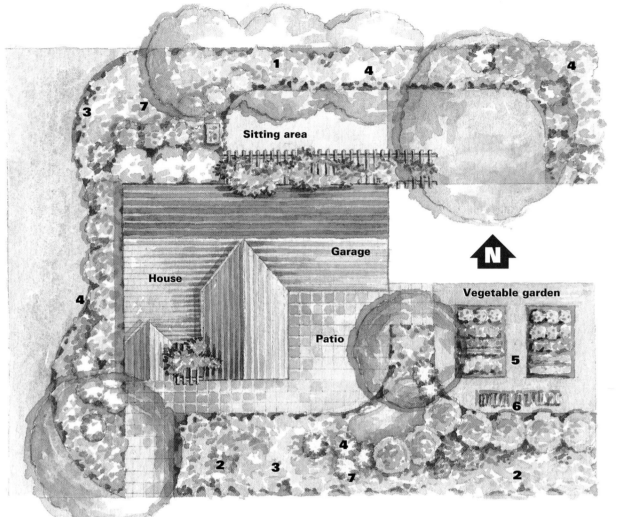

1. *Pears offer tempting fruit.*
2. *Open areas warm up quickly in the morning.*
3. *Plant special patches to view from windows with binoculars.*
4. *Use host plants as ornamentals and hedges.*
5. *Vegetable gardens attract butterflies, too.*
6. *A log pile provides butterfly shelter.*
7. *The more nectar flowers you plant, the better.*

A yard that is welcoming to butterflies will soon attract more individuals, and possibly more species as well. Sunny, open areas of abundant nectar flowers will draw the attention of a growing number of butterflies. Protecting butterflies from strong breezes with hedges and other windbreaks will keep them flying among your flowers in times when they might ordinarily be seeking shelter.

Over time, you will begin to notice which flowers in your garden attract the most butterflies and what species prefer which blossoms. You can then fine-tune your garden beds by adding or replacing plants until you have a mix that best suits your visitors.

As you incorporate more host plants for butterfly larvae, many species are likely to become residents that live out their life cycle right in your garden. It is a delight to notice a number of newly hatched butterflies flitting about your flowers, as they will after hatching from chrysalises hidden in your garden.

By adding fruit trees and fruit feeders, you can make your garden alluring to butterflies that do not depend on nectar. Mud puddles and other water sources will provide the means for moisture-seeking butterflies to indulge in their typical behaviors.

A BOON FOR BUTTERFLIES

Because butterflies are such a pleasure to watch, it's easy to forget that providing for their needs can be extremely beneficial to these flying insects. Butterflies are greatly affected by alteration or destruction of natural habitats. By providing butterflies with a place to feed and raise future generations, you may increase the chances for long-term survival of various species. An abundance of host plants improves the chances for populations to increase. A reliable supply of nectar and other foods in a sheltered garden may also give butterflies an edge in the survival struggle.

ENJOYING BUTTERFLIES

Butterfly gardening will give you hours of enjoyment observing the varieties of butterflies in your garden. It can also lead you to interact more closely with nature as it unfolds in front of you. A daily butterfly journal will help you learn how to enhance your garden and increase your success at attracting and keeping butterflies in your yard. You might also try your hand at butterfly photography or drawing, or expand your activities in other areas.

RAISING BUTTERFLIES

Rearing butterflies from egg to adult, then letting them go (see page 49) is educational and delightful, but be sure to collect your own eggs or larvae rather than purchasing them. The trade in larvae and adult butterflies, which have become popular to release at weddings and other celebrations, can cause problems by introducing non-native species. The larva or adults you import may also introduce diseases or pest organisms that could wreak havoc on wild populations.

JOINING UP

National organizations and local clubs that you can join are a good way to share your enjoyment of butterflies with others and learn more. You may help foster new discoveries or contribute to knowledge about butterflies and

Experiencing the delicate touch of butterfly feet on your hand is a thrill for people of all ages. Observing these creatures and learning more about their habits is the start of a satisfying hobby that can last a lifetime.

the plants they depend on. By providing a sanctuary in your backyard, you help keep butterflies thriving.

FOR FURTHER INFORMATION

Recommended field guides for identification:
A Field Guide to Eastern Butterflies,
    by Paul Opler and Roger Tory Peterson
    (Houghton Mifflin, 1998)
A Field Guide to Western Butterflies,
    by Paul Opler (Houghton Mifflin, 1999)

The following societies offer a large amount of detailed information:
The Lepidopterists' Society, 900 Exposition
    Blvd., Los Angeles, CA 90007. Online:
    www.furman.edu/~snyder/snyder/lep/
National Wildlife Federation Backyard
    Wildlife Habitat Program, 8925 Leesburg
    Pike, Vienna, VA 22184-0001.
    Online: www.nwf.org/habitats
North American Butterfly Association,
    4 Delaware Rd., Morristown, NJ 07960.
    Online: www.naba.org

BUTTERFLY BINOCULARS

A pair of close-focus binoculars is an excellent way to get a close-up look at the butterflies in your garden from a distance that avoids startling your beautiful visitors. Color and pattern are a revelation when magnified, and it is fascinating to watch the butterfly's proboscis probe a flower.

The growing popularity of butterfly-watching has led to the introduction of binocular models designed for magnification at close range. Binoculars with a magnification power of 8 to 10 are ideal. (The magnification power is the first number in binocular specifications—for example, the "10" in "10 × 42".) Try out several styles to make sure you see crisp, bright detail from a distance of just a few feet. Check the Internet and ask friends for recommendations, too.

Practice focusing on particular flowers—with or without butterflies. When you can zoom in on a red zinnia, for example, you'll be able to put the same skills to use when a Tiger Swallowtail is perched atop the flower. A fruit feeder or mud puddle, where butterflies linger for a long time, is a good place to practice.

GALLERY OF BUTTERFLY PLANTS

Butterflies are attracted to flowers of different colors and structure than the flowers that hummingbirds find tempting. Instead of red and orange, butterflies are drawn to purple and yellow. Although they also sip from tubular flowers, they prefer clusters of tiny or small flowers where they can perch while sipping. A few flowers are highly attractive to both butterflies and hummingbirds, such as the Mexican sunflower (*Tithonia rotundifolia*) featured in this gallery, and the butterfly bush (*Buddleia davidii*), discussed here and in the hummingbird gallery on page 34. Butterflies are not as specialized in their needs as hummingbirds, which evolved in the Americas along with many of their favorite nectar plants, so you will find numerous species from other countries included in the gallery, as well as American natives. Many beautiful, easy-to-grow plants will fit your butterfly garden. Butterflies will also visit your garden to seek host plants on which to lay their eggs. By including host plants, you can encourage a growing population of butterflies in your garden. Check the descriptions and information provided in this gallery section, and in the lists on pages 90 and 91, to be sure they will thrive in your climate and growing conditions.

ALCEA ROSEA

al-SEE-uh RO-zee-uh

Hollyhock

5'
2'

Hollyhock (Alcea rosea) provides caterpillar fodder for many species.

- Biennial or perennial in the wild
- Host plant
- Single or double blooms in red, pink, yellow, white, and near-black
- Blooms from early through late summer
- Zones 3 to 8

Tall, stately hollyhocks add a charming, old-fashioned air to the garden. Somewhat coarse up close, they provide a delightful cottage-garden feel to the back of the mixed border or against the wall of a barn or an adobe structure. The spires of ruffled blooms open slowly, from the bottom of the spike to the top, over a period of weeks. Hollyhock leaves are food for the caterpillars of the Painted Lady, West Coast Lady, Northern White-Skipper, and Common Checkered-Skipper.

CULTURE: Sow seeds or place plants in fertile, well-drained garden soil in full sun. Clip off spent flower spikes to encourage more blooms. In the South, plant A. *rugosa*, a species more tolerant of humidity and heat.

RECOMMENDED CULTIVARS: 'Nigra' is a single-flowered, striking deep maroon cultivar that is often sold as a "black" hollyhock. Frilly double-flowered forms are available, such as 'Powderpuff' and 'Chaters Double'.

ANAPHALIS MARGARITACEA

an-uh-FA-liss mar-guh-ree-TAY-see-uh

Pearly everlasting

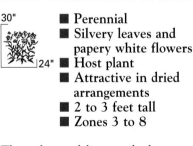
30"
24"

- Perennial
- Silvery leaves and papery white flowers
- Host plant
- Attractive in dried arrangements
- 2 to 3 feet tall
- Zones 3 to 8

The soft gray foliage and white flowers of pearly everlasting add coolness to the garden, combining well with blues, pinks, and other silvery plants. The interesting buttonlike flowers feel stiff and papery to the touch. Stems of leaves and flowers dry easily when hung upside down. Check the plants for green or purplish caterpillars before you cut them: This is one of the host plants of the American Lady, which also eats pussy-toes (*Antennaria* spp.) and other plants.

CULTURE: Sow seeds or place plants in full sun, in average to lean garden soil. Divide plants in early spring to increase your supply.

RECOMMENDED SPECIES: Two similar plants with silvery leaves and clusters of white flowers are also used by the American Lady as host plants. Pussy-toes (*Antennaria* spp.) is good as an edging plant or groundcover in sunny areas. Sweet everlasting (*Gnaphalium* spp.) has flowers that are often sweetly fragrant.

Pearly everlasting bears white papery-crisp blossoms; it's also a host plant of the American Lady.

ARISTOLOCHIA SPP.

uh-riss-toe-LOW-kee-uh

Pipevine

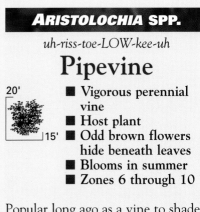

20'

15'

- Vigorous perennial vine
- Host plant
- Odd brown flowers hide beneath leaves
- Blooms in summer
- Zones 6 through 10

Popular long ago as a vine to shade front porches, Dutchman's pipe (*A. macrophylla*) is making a comeback thanks to its striking, bold foliage, carefree nature, and attractiveness to the beautiful Pipevine

Swallowtail, which uses the plant as a caterpillar host. The heart-shaped leaves of the vine are so much in demand by Pipevine Swallowtails that it is believed the species is expanding its range as the garden popularity of the vine increases. Pipevine is the only host plant used by this butterfly. Use it on a trellis or arbor, or to soften a fence.

CULTURE: Place plants in full sun to shade, in average garden soil, at the foot of a permanent support. The deciduous vines need no special care to perform well. Prune back to keep in bounds if necessary.

RECOMMENDED SPECIES: Pipevine Swallowtail larvae use three species of pipevine:

A. macrophylla (Dutchman's pipe), an eastern species; *A. serpentaria* (Virginia snakeroot), native to the Southeast; and *A. californica* (California pipevine).

The big, bold, heart-shaped leaves of Dutchman's pipe signal dinner to Pipevine Swallowtail larvae.

ASCLEPIAS SPP.

uh-SKLEE-pee-us

Milkweed

24"

24"

- Perennials, annuals, and shrubby species
- Excellent nectar and host plants
- Sweet fragrance
- Ideal for meadows
- Zones 2 to 10, depending on species

Only a few milkweeds are well-known to gardeners, but all are familiar to butterflies. These excellent nectar plants come in colors of vivid orange, red, yellow,

pink, purple, white, and green. The Monarch and Queen butterflies seek milkweeds to use as host plants.

CULTURE: Most milkweeds do best in full sun, in well-drained, average to lean garden soil. Pink swamp milkweed (*A. incarnata*) thrives in wet places too; it's a good choice for pondside plantings.

RECOMMENDED SPECIES: Native *A. tuberosa* is a bright, easy-care garden flower; try the rich orange species with blue salvias, or plant cultivars such as 'Gay Butterflies', which includes pink shades as well as orange and yellow. Scarlet milkweed (*A. curassavica*), a bushy, 5-foot-tall South American plant, is an impressive annual. Use

sweet-scented common milkweed (*A. syriaca*) against a fence or building, where its large leaves and architectural form are highlighted and it can spread at will.

A Monarch larva forages on butterfly weed (Asclepias tuberosa).

ASTER SPP.

ASS-ter

Aster

36"

36"

- Easy-care perennials
- White, purple, blue
- Nectar and host
- 1 to 6 feet tall, depending on species
- Blooms summer through late fall
- Zones 2 to 10

Asters are ideal to fill your garden with color late in the season. Their flowers are eagerly sought by nectar-sipping butterflies, and the plants are used as caterpillar fodder by

several species, including the Pearl and Painted Crescents. Use asters in beds, borders, and meadows.

CULTURE: Asters are easy to grow. Many, such as the tall, richly colored New England aster (*A. novae-angliae*) and its cultivars, thrive in full sun; others, including the soft lavender-blue heart-leaved aster (*A. cordifolius*), flourish in shade. Most are highly adaptable to site and conditions. Many self-sow, making them ideal for meadow gardens or natural landscapes.

RECOMMENDED SPECIES: About 150 species are native to North America, most of them beautiful and trouble-free. The tall New England aster (*A. novae-*

angliae) and New York aster (*A. novi-belgii*) have received attention from breeders; the downsized cultivars 'Purple Dome' and pink 'Alma Potschke' are popular.

Asters provide blooms for residents and migrants alike, summer through fall. This aster is 'Purple Dome'.

BUDDLEIA SPP.

BUD-lee-uh

Butterfly bush

6'
5'

Butterfly bush (Buddleia davidii) is always alive with butterflies. It also attracts hummingbirds.

- Deciduous and evergreen shrubs
- Superb nectar for butterflies and hummingbirds
- Long-blooming, late-season flowers
- Zones 5 to 10

Buddleias are constantly humming with nectar sippers, from small insects and wasps to butterflies and hummingbirds. Their tightly packed clusters of tiny, tubular blossoms are superb nectar sources, and their long bloom period guarantees a reliable supply. Butterfly bush (*B. davidii*), discussed in the Gallery of Hummingbird Plants on page 34, is usually one of the first plants to be added to a butterfly garden. Watch for the odd Hummingbird Clearwing moth at buddleia flowers; it hovers and looks like a tiny hummingbird.

CULTURE: *B. davidii* and *B. alternifolia* thrive in full sun in average garden soil. If winter cold kills top growth, or a plant needs to be reinvigorated, cut to ground level in late winter before new growth begins.

RECOMMENDED SPECIES: For butterfly gardens through Zone 5, butterfly bush (*B. davidii*) is a must. Its relative, the purple fountain buddleia (*B. alternifolia*), is a good choice for butterfly gardens in cold-winter areas.

CEANOTHUS SPP.

see-uh-NO-thiss

California lilac

3'
8'

Nectar-rich California lilac is popular with western butterflies, several of which use it as a host plant.

- Deciduous and evergreen shrubs
- Airy puffs of blue or white flowers
- Nectar and host
- 1 to 15 feet tall
- Spring bloom
- Zones 7 to 10, depending on species

California lilac is a popular native garden plant in the West. Species and hybrids range in height and habit from low-growing groundcovers to large, treelike shrubs. They flower mainly in blue and white. Many butterflies, especially western species, use the plants as hosts, including the Brown Elfin, Spring Azure, Pale Swallowtail, California Hairstreak, California Tortoiseshell, and others. The large golden brown Ceanothus Silkmoth also uses ceanothus as a host. Both butterflies and hummingbirds may nectar at the plants.

CULTURE: Plant in full sun in very well-drained soil. Most species are not winter-hardy in cold regions. Many are attractive to deer.

RECOMMENDED SPECIES: Some 50 species and many improved cultivars are available. Creamy white-flowered New Jersey tea (*C. americanus*) is an eastern native that is cold-hardy to Zone 4.

ECHINACEA PURPUREA

ek-ih-NAY-see-uh pur-PUR-ee-uh

Purple coneflower

36"
24"
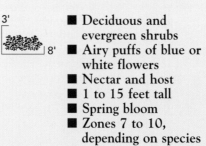

Purple coneflower is a staple because of its success in attracting swallowtails and other butterflies.

- Easy-care perennial
- Nectar plant
- Early summer through fall bloom
- 2 to 4 feet tall
- Zones 3 to 8

A workhorse of the perennial garden or in prairie and meadow plantings, purple coneflower is highly appealing to nectar-seeking butterflies because of its generous-size daisy flowers and purple color. Finches and other small songbirds visit to eat ripe seeds of this native wildflower. Flower centers form a raised cone of glowing orange. The tawny Ottoe Skipper uses *E. purpurea* as a nectar plant.

CULTURE: Purple coneflower is one of the easiest perennials to grow. Sow seeds or settle plants in full sun in average to fertile, well-drained soil. Drought-tolerant. May self-sow in moderation.

RECOMMENDED SPECIES: The species is ideal for butterflies. 'Bright Star' has intense color. 'White Swan' has less initial appeal because its flowers are white rather than purple. 'Magnus' has huge flat flowers with brilliant color. *E. pallida* is a pale purple-pink. *E. angustifolia*, native farther west and north, has pink flowers and a flat center. *E. tennesseensis* is listed as an endangered species in the wild but grows well in gardens.

EUPATORIUM SPP.

yew-puh-TOR-ee-um

Joe-Pye weed

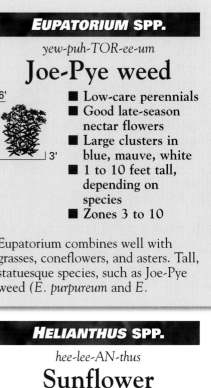

6'
3'

- Low-care perennials
- Good late-season nectar flowers
- Large clusters in blue, mauve, white
- 1 to 10 feet tall, depending on species
- Zones 3 to 10

Eupatorium combines well with grasses, coneflowers, and asters. Tall, statuesque species, such as Joe-Pye weed (*E. purpureum* and *E. maculatum*), are a bold presence in the garden. Shorter ones, such as white snakeroot (*Ageratina altissima*) and the spreading blue mistflower or hardy ageratum (*Conoclinium coelestinum*), are best for wild gardens where they can roam. Many are native to the East. All are nectar plants sought by butterflies and other insects.

CULTURE: Plant in full sun to part shade, in average garden soil. Some species, including Joe-Pye weed and boneset (*E. perfoliatum*), also thrive in wet locations.

RECOMMENDED SPECIES: Find room for giant Joe-Pye weed or its downsized cultivars, 'Gateway' and 'Glow', which top out at about 5 feet. Mistflower (*Conoclinium coelestinum*) cultivars of note include the blue 'Cori' and 'Wayside Variety', and white 'Album'.

Joe-Pye weed is a big presence that is irresistible to butterflies. This cultivar is Eupatorium × 'Gateway'.

HELIANTHUS SPP.

hee-lee-AN-thus

Sunflower

8'
3'

- Perennials and annuals
- Cheerful golden daisies
- May spread vigorously
- Nectar and host plants
- 2 to 15 feet tall
- Zone 2 to 9; annuals all zones

Tall *H. annuus* and its decorative cultivars are just the beginning of this genus, which also includes many sturdy, often fast-spreading perennials. All are American natives. Plant them in wildflower meadows or in natural borders with native grasses and late-blooming perennials. All are highly attractive nectar sources for butterflies.

CULTURE: Plant in full sun in lean to average soil. Some, such as woodland sunflower (*H. strumosus*), also thrive in shade. Sunflowers can be invasive. Most are fairly easy to pull up, but Jerusalem artichoke (*H. tuberosus*) has brittle roots that break into pieces and regrow rapidly. Annual species reseed.

RECOMMENDED SPECIES: The many annual sunflower cultivars could fill a garden. Perennials include Maximilian sunflower (*H. maximilianii*), with willowlike leaves on supertall stems; soft sunflower (*H. mollis*), with velvety leaves and relaxed stems; and sawtooth sunflower (*H. grosse-seriatus*), which forms an expanding clump of tall stems covered in flowers.

Maximilian sunflower is best in natural gardens where its fast-spreading roots can have free rein.

HELIOTROPIUM ARBORESCENS

hee-lee-oh-TROH-pee-um ar-bor-ESS-ens

Heliotrope

20"
12"

- Tender shrub usually grown as annual
- Legendary vanilla-like fragrance
- Outstanding rich, deep purple color
- Summer through frost
- Hardy in Zone 10; as annual, all zones

An old favorite, heliotrope is familiar to most gardeners as a bedding annual, but it is actually a Peruvian shrub that can reach 6 feet tall. Butterflies are drawn to the large clusters of many small flowers, which boast a heady fragrance and a beautiful color.

CULTURE: Plant in fertile, moisture-retentive soil in full sun. Combine with perennials and annuals, or plant in pots for deck and patio.

RECOMMENDED CULTIVARS: Plants vary widely in the quality of their aroma; if you're buying plants as annuals, with flowers already opening, sniff before you buy. 'Marine' has extra-large flower clusters on 18-inch plants; 'Mini-Marine' is a compact, 8-inch-tall version. 'Regale Dwarf' is another shorty, good in window boxes or other containers.

Heliotrope (Heliotropium arborescens 'Marine') uses sweet scent and purple color to tempt a Clouded Sulphur.

HIBISCUS SPP.

hi-BIS-kus

Hibiscus

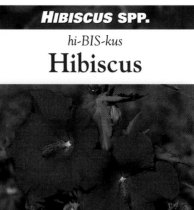

Hibiscus 'Lord Baltimore' brings butterflies and hummingbirds to its huge, nectar-rich flowers.

5'
3'

- Perennials, shrubs, or trees
- Tropical ambience
- Good patio plants
- Attract butterflies and hummingbirds
- Many cold-tender; a few hardy species
- Zones 5 to 10

Big, splashy blooms are what attract gardeners, butterflies, and hummingbirds to hibiscus. Use these decorative shrubs and small trees to anchor a flower bed or flank a gate, or even as a flowering hedge. Tender species are often sold as outdoor potted plants in summer in the North; they flourish in pots and provide weeks of color.

CULTURE: Plant in full sun in well-drained soil, or grow in large containers. Most tender species are hardy only to Zone 10 but can be overwintered indoors in bright light.

RECOMMENDED SPECIES: Rose mallow (*H. moscheutos*), a perennial hardy to Zone 5, has immense flowers in red, pink, rose, and white; 'Southern Belle' and 'Disco Belle' are popular strains. Chinese hibiscus (*H. rosa-sinensis*) is a tender shrub or small tree hardy in Zone 10, useful as a patio plant in the North. Rose-of sharon (*H. syriacus*), hardy to Zone 5, has blue-lavender, white, or reddish-purple blooms on a shrub or small tree.

LIATRIS SPP.

lye-AH-tris

Blazing star

Prairie blazing star (Liatris pycnostachya), graced by an Eastern Tiger Swallowtail.

36"
24"

- Adaptable, easy perennial
- Fuzzy spikes of rosy purple flowers
- 1 to 3 feet tall
- Summer to fall bloom
- Zones 3 to 9

Liatris is an American wildflower that is also a hit in the cut-flower trade. Its flowers open from the top of the spike to the bottom and bloom for weeks in the garden. They are a magnet for butterflies, especially swallowtails. Under garden conditions, the plants often grow taller than they do in their wild habitats, where they may be found in prairies, on rocky ledges, and in poor, dry soil. Liatris is a good partner for purple coneflower.

CULTURE: Plant the bulblike tuberous roots in spring, or set potted plants into the garden in well-drained soil in full sun. You can also grow liatris from seed; it takes a year to flower.

RECOMMENDED SPECIES: Thirty-five species of liatris are native to North America, but only a few have found their way into nurseries. Most common is *L. spicata* and its cultivar 'Kobold' (also called 'Gnome'), with stout rosy purple flower spikes. *L. punctata* is especially drought-tolerant. *L. pycnostachya* is a late bloomer that grows over 3 feet tall.

LINDERA BENZOIN

LIN-der-uh BEN-zo-in

Spicebush

Delightfully scented spicebush (Lindera benzoin) is a host plant for the Spicebush Swallowtail.

10'
10'

- Graceful shrub for shade
- Yellow flowers on bare branches in early spring
- Delightful, spicy scent
- Host plant
- Zones 5 to 8

This eastern North America native shrub is a fine choice for a shady butterfly garden. It has a graceful, somewhat horizontal branching pattern, producing an attractive winter silhouette. The pleasant, medicinal scent is released when its foliage, flowers, berries, and twigs are crushed between the fingers. In early spring, its yellow flowers brighten the woodland understory or shade garden. In fall, its leaves gleam soft golden yellow, accented by glossy red berries. Spicebush Swallowtail uses it as a host plant; so does the large, velvety brown Promethea Silkmoth. It may take some detective work to find the swallowtail caterpillars, as they conceal themselves in rolled leaves. If you notice chewed foliage, look closely to find the larvae.

CULTURE: Plant in well-drained or moist soil, well enriched with chopped, dry leaves or other humus. Grows fast to attain eventual height of 10 feet. Additional shoots often spring up near the trunk.

LIRIODENDRON TULIPIFERA

leer-ee-oh-DEN-drun
too-lih-PIH-fur-uh

Tulip tree

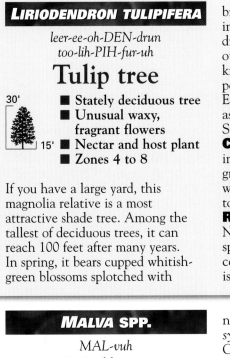

30'

- Stately deciduous tree
- Unusual waxy, fragrant flowers
- Nectar and host plant
- Zones 4 to 8

15'

If you have a large yard, this magnolia relative is a most attractive shade tree. Among the tallest of deciduous trees, it can reach 100 feet after many years. In spring, it bears cupped whitish-green blossoms splotched with bright orange and green at the base; in fall, it holds many seeds, which draw grosbeaks, goldfinches, and other seedeaters. Tulip tree, also known as tulip poplar or yellow poplar, is a host plant for the Eastern Tiger Swallowtail, as well as the large, dark brown Promethea Silkmoth and Tuliptree Silkmoth.

CULTURE: Plant in sun to shade, in humus-enriched soil. Easy to grow from seed. Transplant seedlings when young (about 6 inches tall) to avoid damaging the taproot.

RECOMMENDED CULTIVARS: None are improvements on the species where butterflies are concerned. 'Arnold' ('Fastigiatum') is a narrowly columnar cultivar.

Tulip tree (Liriodendron tulipifera), a large shade tree, hosts caterpillars of the Eastern Tiger Swallowtail.

MALVA SPP.

MAL-vuh

Mallow

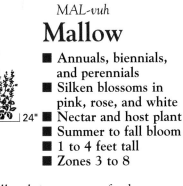

30"

- Annuals, biennials, and perennials
- Silken blossoms in pink, rose, and white
- Nectar and host plant
- Summer to fall bloom
- 1 to 4 feet tall
- Zones 3 to 8

24"

Mallow brings waves of color to the garden, with hollyhock-like blossoms held on bushy, branching plants. The flowers are used by butterflies and hummingbirds for nectar. Mallows, including M. *sylvestris*, are host plants for West Coast Lady, Tropical Checkered-Skipper, and Common Sootywing.

CULTURE: Plant seeds or place plants in full sun, in average to poor, well-drained soil. Drought-tolerant.

RECOMMENDED CULTIVARS: *Malva alcea* 'Fastigiata' displays lovely pink blooms from summer through frost; at up to 4 feet tall, this bushy plant is stunning in the garden. Pristine white M. *moschata* 'Alba' is beautiful in an all-white garden or among blue and red salvias; 'Rosea' is a deep pink. *Malva sylvestris* also offers abundant flowers; cultivars include old-fashioned 'Zebrina', with small, striped pinkish-purple flowers.

Malva sylvestris 'Zebrina' has stems lined with perky nectar flowers from early summer through frost.

ORIGANUM VULGARE

o-RIG-uh-num vul-GER-ee

Common oregano

24"

- Sprawling, spreading perennial
- Masses of pinkish-lavender flowers
- Superb nectar plant
- Blooms summer through early fall
- Zones 5 to 10

24"

Oregano is not only for the kitchen. It's first-rate in the butterfly garden, too, where it will attract many swallowtails and other species, along with a myriad of other nectar-seeking insects. This trouble-free perennial roots along its stems to expand into an ever-larger planting, which makes it a good choice for growing on a sunny bank, atop a wall, or in a raised bed where it can roam at will.

CULTURE: Start seeds in pots (seedlings are tiny) or settle plants into a site with full sun, in average to poor soil. Drought-tolerant. Strays are easy to pull up; replant to extend the planting elsewhere, or pass them along to friends.

The aroma of the leaves is crucial when you're growing oregano for seasoning, but butterflies adore the flowers no matter how weak the "true oregano" smell of the foliage.

RECOMMENDED CULTIVARS: The hybrid cultivar 'Kent Beauty' (zones 5 to 8) and O. *laevigatum* 'Herrenhausen' (zones 7 to 10) are very attractive to butterflies.

The hybrid oregano cultivar 'Kent Beauty' and, inset, Origanum laevigatum 'Herrenhausen'.

PASSIFLORA SPP.

pass-ih-FLOR-uh

Passionflower

**Passionflower (Passiflora × 'Incense')
looks like a finicky exotic, but it's
easy to grow and a good host plant.**

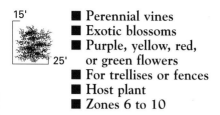
15'
25'

- Perennial vines
- Exotic blossoms
- Purple, yellow, red, or green flowers
- For trellises or fences
- Host plant
- Zones 6 to 10

It's the Passion of Christ that gives this unusual flower its name. Each part of the flower is symbolic of the event, from the "cross" made by the pistil to the "crown of thorns" at the base of the petals. Vines are vigorous and fast-growing, which makes them good candidates for a trellis or an arbor, or to cover a fence. They bear aromatic fruits. Several brilliantly colored

butterflies use species of *Passiflora* as a host plant, including the Gulf Fritillary, Julia, and Zebra.
CULTURE: Most passionflower species do well in full sun in average soil and are drought-tolerant. Prune back as needed to keep in bounds. Suckers may arise from roots away from parent plant; mow or clip off if desired.
RECOMMENDED SPECIES: For a hardy species that thrives to Zone 6, try *P. incarnata*, the purple passionflower, also known as maypop. Argentinian *P. caerulea* has beautiful blue flowers. *P. foetida*, a white-flowered species, bears yellow to red fruits and is a favorite of the Mexican Fritillary.

PETROSELINUM CRISPUM

peh-tross-uh-LI-num KRIS-pum

Parsley

**Parsley (Petroselinum crispum) is
favored by the Black Swallowtail as
a host plant.**

12"
15"

- Aromatic biennial or perennial herb
- Good as edging for flower beds
- Host plant
- Foliage more valuable than flowers
- Zones 2 to 10

Grow parsley in your garden for its ruffled, curly leaves (or smooth, ferny leaves) and its neat, mounded shape. But don't get too attached to your plants, because they are likely to become food for the vivid green-and-black-striped caterpillars of the Black Swallowtail, as well as the Anise Swallowtail of the West. These butterflies are so common a

pest of parsley that their caterpillars were once scorned as "parsley worms." When you see adult butterflies flying low near the plants, look closely for the small, pearl-like eggs, usually laid singly here and there on leaves or stems.
CULTURE: Parsley is slow to germinate; start seed in pots. Or place plants in full sun, in fertile to average, well-drained soil. Should plants become shabby, cut back to ground level to encourage a flush of new growth.
RECOMMENDED CULTIVARS: Both flat and curly parsley are appealing to the Black and Anise Swallowtails, and any cultivar or unnamed variety will be welcomed.

RUDBECKIA SPP.

rud-BEK-ee-a

Black-eyed Susan

**Black-eyed Susan (Rudbeckia spp.)
offers many tiny, nectar-filled, petal-
less flowers in its dark centers.**

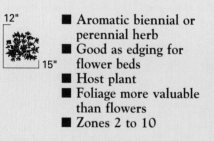
30"
18"

- Perennials, biennials, annuals
- Dark-centered golden daisies
- Nectar and host
- Blooms summer to fall
- 1 to 10 feet tall
- Zones 3 to 9; annuals, all zones

This genus of North American natives includes many fine species and cultivars, some of them not an improvement from a butterfly point of view. The popular 'Goldsturm', for instance, has little appeal as a nectar flower. Green-headed coneflower (*R. laciniata*) is a host

plant for the Silvery Checkerspot.
CULTURE: All rudbeckias are easy to grow. Set plants in well-drained soil, in full sun. *R. subtomentosa* also flourishes in part to full shade.
RECOMMENDED SPECIES: Green-headed coneflower (*R. laciniata*) grows to 10 feet; it's an excellent choice for meadows, prairie gardens, and the back of the border. Often behaving as biennials, the bright Gloriosa daisy (*R. hirta* cultivars), as well as the species *R. hirta*, are short-lived but floriferous and beautiful with asters, salvias, and grasses. Small-flowered but profuse, *R. subtomentosa* is popular as a nectar source with small butterflies such as crescents.

SCABIOSA CAUCASICA

skab-ee-OH-suh kaw-KAY-sih-ka

Pincushion flower

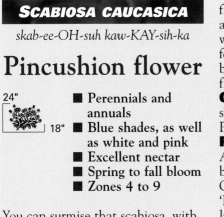

24"
18"
- Perennials and annuals
- Blue shades, as well as white and pink
- Excellent nectar
- Spring to fall bloom
- Zones 4 to 9

You can surmise that scabiosa, with cultivar names such as 'Butterfly Blue', is highly appealing to nectar-seeking butterflies. It may also be visited by hummingbirds. The flowers are held on bare stems above a neat mound of foliage, which makes these plants excellent for edging beds and borders. They bloom for months, pushing up new flower buds from spring through fall. **CULTURE:** Grow in full sun to light shade, in average, well-drained soil. Perennials may be short-lived. **RECOMMENDED CULTIVARS:** All cultivars are welcomed by butterflies. Good blues include 'Blue Cockade', 'Blue Moon', 'Fama', and 'Perfecta'. The dwarf 'Pink Mist' is lavender. For purple flowers that are appealing to butterflies, try 'Perfecta Lilac'. 'Alba' is white-flowered. The annual *S. atropurpurea* is also a good nectar flower.

Scabiosa *'Butterfly Blue'* has a fitting name: Like other scabiosas, it's a highly popular nectar flower.

SEDUM 'AUTUMN JOY'

SEE-dum

'Autumn Joy' sedum

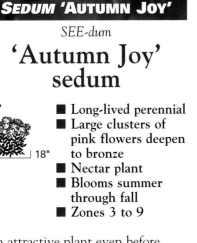

24"
18"
- Long-lived perennial
- Large clusters of pink flowers deepen to bronze
- Nectar plant
- Blooms summer through fall
- Zones 3 to 9

An attractive plant even before bloom, 'Autumn Joy' transforms itself into a mass of flowers in summer and looks good right through winter, with its clustered flower heads punctuating the garden. It is absolutely magnetic to nectaring butterflies and is easy to grow in the garden or in containers. Flowers begin pale pink, deepen to salmon pink, and finally acquire a reddish-bronze autumn hue. **CULTURE:** Set plants in almost any garden soil, from dry to wet areas, in full sun. Highly adaptable. Grows into an expanding clump. Excellent in containers. **RECOMMENDED CULTIVARS:** 'Autumn Joy' is a hybrid sedum, a cross of *S. spectabile* and the related *Hylotelephium telephium*. It is a top-notch plant, both for ease of growing and appeal to butterflies. For a more dramatic color, try 'Meteor', another hybrid of the same parentage, which has large flower heads of glowing pink that gradually turn to deep red.

The late-blooming flowers of Sedum 'Autumn Joy' provide nectar for many species of butterflies.

SOLIDAGO SPP.

so-li-DAY-go

Goldenrod

36"
18"
- Perennials
- Nectar and host
- Blooms summer through fall
- Zones 2 to 10

A familiar field flower, goldenrod brightens wild gardens where its often spreading roots are free to roam. It is ideal for meadows and prairies and alongside fences, barns, and other outbuildings. The glowing yellow flowers are not responsible for allergies: Their pollen is transferred by insects (which visit the flowers in huge numbers), not by the wind. The western *S. californica* is a host for Northern Checkerspot; *S. radiata* is preferred by the Rockslide Checkerspot. **CULTURE:** Plant these tough, easy-care perennials in poor to average soil, in full sun. Drought-tolerant. *S. caesia, S. flexicaulis,* and a few other species also flourish in shade. **RECOMMENDED SPECIES:** Most of the 100 or so species of goldenrod are native to North America. Learn your local representatives of this genus, which will be well-suited for your climate and conditions. Downsized, clump-forming cultivars, such as 'Golden Baby' and 'Golden Fleece', are available for more controlled beds and borders.

Goldenrods are excellent in a meadow, where they can spread. This one is 'Golden Fleece'.

TITHONIA ROTUNDIFOLIA

tih-THONE-ee-uh
ro-TUN-dih-FOH-lee-uh

Mexican sunflower

The vivid blossoms of Mexican sunflower (Tithonia rotundifolia) draw butterflies and hummingbirds.

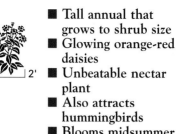
6'
2'

- Tall annual that grows to shrub size
- Glowing orange-red daisies
- Unbeatable nectar plant
- Also attracts hummingbirds
- Blooms midsummer to fall
- All zones

As a focal point in the garden, tithonia is unbeatable for both humans and butterflies, especially the Monarch and swallowtails. It also shines like a beacon to hummingbirds, which share the nectar with butterflies and other insects. Partner this bushy annual with blue flowers such as salvia or with late-blooming asters in shades of blue and purple. It also holds its own among other hot colors, such as red, orange, and yellow. The stems are as soft as velvet.

CULTURE: Easy to grow. Sow seeds in full sun, in well-drained, average to poor soil. May self-sow.

RECOMMENDED CULTIVARS: The species can grow to 8 feet. Shorter 'Torch' reaches about 6 feet; 'Goldfinger' tops out at about 4 feet. 'Fiesta del Sol' is a new selection that is the shortest of all, growing only 2 to 3 feet high.

VERBENA SPP.

ver-BEE-nuh

Verbenas

Verbena bonariensis *is irresistible to nectar-seeking Monarchs.*

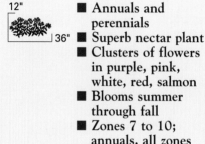
12"
36"

- Annuals and perennials
- Superb nectar plant
- Clusters of flowers in purple, pink, white, red, salmon
- Blooms summer through fall
- Zones 7 to 10; annuals, all zones

Verbena is among the best nectar flowers you can grow for nonstop bloom that keeps butterflies lingering in the garden. Use tall species in perennial beds and cottage gardens and low growers in front of beds, to edge walks and patios, and in containers.

CULTURE: Plant in full sun in well-drained, average to lean soil. Drought-tolerant.

RECOMMENDED SPECIES: *V. bonariensis* is a short-lived perennial with open stems 4 feet tall topped by mauve-purple flower clusters; it often reseeds itself prolifically. *V. tenuisecta* is a low, spreading species, excellent as a groundcover. *V. canadensis* is another prostrate species with rosy purple flowers. Many hybrid cultivars are available; 'Peaches and Cream' and 'Apple Blossom' are delicate pastels; 'Sparkle Hybrids' have strong, clear colors. 'Homestead Purple' is a low-growing, carefree perennial that no butterfly garden should be without.

VERNONIA SPP.

ver-NO-nee-uh

Ironweed

New York ironweed (Vernonia noveboracensis) has rich color that signals nectar to butterflies from late summer through fall.

6'
2'

- Foolproof perennials
- Intense, deep purple flowers in clusters
- Excellent late-season nectar plant
- Grows to 6 feet tall
- Zones 4 to 8

Dramatic, deep color draws butterflies, especially swallowtails and the Monarch. Use in the back of a border or in meadow or prairie gardens. Combine with perennial asters, goldenrod, or tithonia for striking color combinations. Bloom begins in midsummer and continues through fall.

CULTURE: Plant in full sun in well-drained to moist soil. May self-sow.

For more blooms, snip off the tops of each stem beneath the first set of leaves when the stems reach about 12 inches tall. This will encourage branching, and each side branch will produce more flowers. The plants often lose the lower leaves; plant shorter nectar flowers in front to mask their leggy looks. The eastern species *V. fasciculata* is tolerant of clay soils.

RECOMMENDED SPECIES: The attractive *V. noveboracensis* is an eastern and southeastern native. Another eastern species, *V. fasciculata*, is also beautiful and long-blooming. Shorter *V. acaulis* is an eastern coastal native.

VIOLA SPP.

vy-OH-luh

Violet

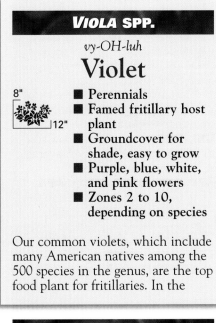

8"

12"

- Perennials
- Famed fritillary host plant
- Groundcover for shade, easy to grow
- Purple, blue, white, and pink flowers
- Zones 2 to 10, depending on species

Our common violets, which include many American natives among the 500 species in the genus, are the top food plant for fritillaries. In the garden, violets are easily tucked into all kinds of niches: as edgings, as sweeps of color in shade or sun, as companions for spring woodland wildflowers, and as low-care groundcovers. The Variegated, Diana, Regal, Great Basin, Pacific, Great Spangled Fritillary and many others use violets as host plants. **CULTURE:** Simple to grow and trouble-free. There is a violet species for just about any garden; follow supplier's instructions for site and conditions. Violets increase by self-sowing or spreading roots. **RECOMMENDED SPECIES:** Bird's-foot violet (*V. pedata*) is a gorgeous, large-flowered blue species. Confederate violet (*V. sororaria*) combines pale gray and deep blue in its profuse flowers. A northern species, *V. labradorica*, has interesting purplish leaves. *V. pubescens* and *V. canadensis* are especially fast spreaders.

Bird's-foot violet (Viola pedata) is one of hundreds of native violets sought as host plants by fritillaries.

VITEX AGNUS-CASTUS

VI-tex AG-nuss CASS-tuss

Chaste tree, Vitex

15'

20'

- Small tree with blue flowers
- Sometimes called summer lilac
- Excellent nectar plant
- To 15 feet
- Zones 6 to 10

Use chaste tree as a small specimen tree or as the centerpiece of your butterfly garden, surrounded by phlox and other nectar flowers. It flourishes in coastal gardens. The elongated clusters of blue flowers are attractive to butterflies, other insects, and hummingbirds. The flowers have a spicy fragrance, and the palm-shaped leaves with silvery undersides are aromatic. In addition to butterflies, the nectar-rich blossoms attract many other fascinating insects. **CULTURE:** Plant in full sun. If top growth is winter-killed, cut back to just above ground level; vitex will bloom the same year on new growth. You can also keep vitex to shrub size of about 6 feet tall by pruning it to ground level in spring. **RECOMMENDED SPECIES:** *V. agnus-castus latifolia* is more cold-hardy and has larger leaves. Flower color may vary in nursery stock from pale blue-purple to a deep, rich hue. To make sure you get the color you want, buy the plant in bloom.

Chaste tree (Vitex agnus-castus) is a good choice as a windbreak in seaside or other gardens.

ZINNIA ELEGANS

ZIN-ee-uh (ZEEN-ee-uh) EL-ih-gans

Zinnia

24"

8"

- Super easy annuals
- Electric bright colors and soft pastels
- Nectar plant
- Blooms summer through fall
- All zones

A longtime favorite garden flower, zinnia is outstanding for attracting butterflies. Hummingbirds also seek nectar from zinnias, particularly those with red and orange flowers. Zinnias are quick to bloom from seed and are available in heights from giants to dwarfs. Butterflies, from large swallowtails to fast-flying skippers, find their nectar tempting. **CULTURE:** Plant seeds in full sun, in average to lean, well-drained soil. Zinnias bloom in about seven weeks from seed. Whitish mildew may disfigure foliage; it is not fatal. To hide mildew-affected leaves, plant shorter flowers, such as blue 'Victoria' salvia, in front. **RECOMMENDED SPECIES:** Any *Z. elegans* cultivar or unnamed variety will be welcomed by butterflies. Red and orange cultivars, such as 'Red Sun', 'Big Red', 'Scarlet Flame', and 'Orange King', also have good hummingbird appeal. Other zinnia species, such as small-flowered, low-growing *Z. angustifolia* and *Z. haageana*, also attract butterflies.

Zinnias attract a constant stream of butterfly guests, such as this Black Swallowtail.

ADDITIONAL BUTTERFLY PLANTS BY REGION

Achillea *'Coronation Gold'*

Pentas *with Monarch*

Echium *with Monarch*

Snapdragon *'Ribbon' mix*

Bidens ferulifolia

Verbena *hybrid with Eastern Tiger Swallowtail*

Expand your butterfly garden by choosing butterfly favorites from these lists to add to your plantings. You'll find many excellent choices for all regions, including nectar plants for adult butterflies and host plants for larvae. Use the shrubs, vines, and trees on these lists to create a permanent structure for your butterfly garden and provide butterflies with a reliable source of nectar and egg-laying sites. Perennial flowers are popular choices with butterfly gardeners, both in flower beds and in meadow gardens and other natural plantings, because they generally get bigger and better every year. Fill in gaps among permanent plants with selections from the list of annuals.

In addition to these lists, there are many other plants suitable for butterflies. Feel free to experiment with other plants that you think will attract nectaring butterflies. Once you begin looking for larvae on your garden plants, you may also discover other host plants that butterflies seek out. Remember that the purpose of host plants is to provide food for caterpillars. Chewed foliage is a sign that your butterfly garden is working and signals an opportunity to enjoy observing the fascinating butterfly life cycle at close range.

NORTHEAST & MIDWEST

NECTAR
Astilbe *(Astilbe* spp.)
Blue spirea *(Caryopteris* spp.)
Boltonia *(Boltonia asteroides)*
Candytuft *(Iberis sempervirens)*
Chives *(Allium schoenoprasum)*
Coneflower *(Ratibida* spp.)
Coreopsis *(Coreopsis* spp.)
Fleabane *(Erigeron* spp.)
Lavender *(Lavandula* spp.)
Lilac *(Syringa* spp.)
Milkweed *(Asclepias* spp.)
Phlox *(Phlox* spp.)
Pinks *(Dianthus* spp.)
Sage *(Salvia* spp.)
Shasta daisy *(Leucanthemum* spp.)
Stoke's aster *(Stokesia* spp.)
Yarrow *(Achillea* spp.)

HOST
Birch *(Betula* spp.)
Blueberry *(Vaccinium* spp.)
Cherry and plum *(Prunus* spp.)
Clover *(Trifolium* spp.)
Crabapple *(Malus* spp.)
Dogwood *(Cornus* spp.)
Elm *(Ulmus* spp.)
Hackberry *(Celtis* spp.)
Hops *(Humulus* spp.)
Milkweed *(Asclepias* spp.)
Nettle *(Urtica* spp.)
Poplar; cottonwood *(Populus* spp.)
Queen Anne's lace *(Daucus carota* spp.)
Turtlehead *(Chelone* spp.)
Willow *(Salix* spp.)
Wisteria *(Wisteria* spp.)

WEST

NECTAR
Agapanthus *(Agapanthus* spp.)
Buckwheat *(Eriogonum* spp.)
Catmint *(Nepeta* spp.)
Cupid's dart *(Catananche caerulea)*
Fleabane *(Erigeron* spp.)
Grapeholly *(Mahonia* spp.)
Hebe *(Hebe* spp.)
Knapweed *(Centaurea* spp.)
Lavender *(Lavandula* spp.)
Lobelia *(Lobelia* spp.)
Lupine *(Lupinus* spp.)
Milkweed *(Asclepias* spp.)
Monkey flower *(Mimulus* spp.)
Penstemon *(Penstemon* spp.)
Pride of Madeira *(Echium fastuosum)*
Sage; salvia *(Salvia* spp.)
Wallflower *(Erysimum cheiri)*

HOST
Azalea *(Rhododendron* spp.)
Buckwheat *(Eriogonum* spp.)
Cherry and plum *(Prunus* spp.)
Fennel *(Foeniculum vulgare)*
Gooseberry; currant *(Ribes* spp.)
Hackberry *(Celtis* spp.)
Lupine *(Lupinus* spp.)
Madrone *(Arbutus menziesii)*
Milkweed *(Asclepias* spp.)
Nettle *(Urtica* spp.)
Oak *(Quercus* spp.)
Penstemon *(Penstemon* spp.)
Pine *(Pinus* spp.)
Poplar; cottonwood *(Populus* spp.)
Toadflax *(Linaria* spp.)
Willow *(Salix* spp.)

ANNUALS FOR ALL REGIONS

Ageratum *(Ageratum houstonianum)*
Annual phlox *(Phlox drummondii)*
Bachelor's button *(Centaurea cyanus)*
Blanket flower *(Gaillardia pulchella)*
Borage *(Borago officinalis)*
China aster *(Callistephus chinensis)*
Cosmos *(Cosmos spp.)*
Dahlia *(Dahlia spp.)*
Dill *(Anethum graveolens)*
Fennel *(Foeniculum spp.)*
Forget-me-not *(Myosotis spp.)*
Globe amaranth *(Gomphrena spp.)*
Impatiens *(Impatiens walleriana)*
Marigold *(Tagetes spp.)*
Nasturtium *(Nasturtium spp.)*
Parsley *(Petroselinum spp.)*
Pentas *(Pentas spp.)*
Petunia *(Petunia spp.)*
Pinks *(Dianthus spp.)*
Snapdragon *(Antirrhinum spp.)*
Snow-on-the-mountain *(Euphorbia marginata)*
Sweet alyssum *(Lobularia maritima)*
Sweet pea *(Lathyrus odoratus)*
Tickseed *(Bidens spp.)*
Verbena *(Verbena spp.)*

Chives with Eastern Tiger Swallowtail

Blue spirea with Anise Swallowtail

SOUTHWEST

NECTAR
Blanket flower *(Gaillardia spp.)*
Blue spirea *(Caryopteris spp.)*
Bouvardia *(Bouvardia spp.)*
California fuchsia *(Epilobium spp.)*
Clover *(Trifolium spp.)*
Coneflower *(Ratibida spp.)*
Coreopsis *(Coreopsis spp.)*
Globe thistle *(Echinops spp.)*
Knapweed *(Centaurea spp.)*
Lupine *(Lupinus spp.)*
Milkweed *(Asclepias spp.)*
Monkey flower *(Mimulus spp.)*
Penstemon *(Penstemon spp.)*
Red hot poker *(Kniphofia spp.)*
Red valerian *(Centranthus ruber spp.)*
Tree tobacco *(Nicotiana glauca)*
Yarrow *(Achillea spp.)*

HOST
Buckwheat *(Eriogonum spp.)*
Cherry and plum *(Prunus spp.)*
Citrus *(Citrus spp.)*
Clover *(Trifolium spp.)*
Gooseberry; currant *(Ribes spp.)*
Hackberry *(Celtis spp.)*
Hawthorn *(Crataegus spp.)*
Hibiscus *(Hibiscus spp.)*
Lupine *(Lupinus spp.)*
Milkweed *(Asclepias spp.)*
Oak *(Quercus spp.)*
Penstemon *(Penstemon spp.)*
Poplar; cottonwood *(Populus spp.)*
Serviceberry *(Amelanchier spp.)*
Sycamore *(Platanus spp.)*
Willow *(Salix spp.)*

SOUTHEAST

NECTAR
Abelia; glossy abelia *(Abelia spp.)*
Astilbe *(Astilbe spp.)*
Blue spirea *(Caryopteris spp.)*
Boltonia *(Boltonia asteroides)*
Cardinal flower *(Lobelia cardinalis)*
Catmint *(Nepeta spp.)*
Chives *(Allium schoenoprasum)*
Daylily *(Hemerocallis spp.)*
Lantana *(Lantana spp.)*
Lobelia *(Lobelia spp.)*
Milkweed *(Asclepias spp.)*
Pentas *(Pentas spp.)*
Phlox *(Phlox spp.)*
Rosemary *(Rosmarinus officinalis)*
Spirea *(Spiraea spp.)*
Summersweet *(Clethra alnifolia)*
Yarrow *(Achillea spp.)*

HOST
Blueberry *(Vaccinium spp.)*
Cherry and plum *(Prunus spp.)*
Citrus *(Citrus spp.)*
Croton *(Codiaeum variegatum pictum)*
Hackberry *(Celtis spp.)*
Hibiscus *(Hibiscus spp.)*
Hops *(Humulus spp.)*
Milkweed *(Asclepias spp.)*
Pawpaw *(Asimina triloba)*
Plantain *(Plantago spp.)*
Queen Anne's lace *(Daucus carota)*
Rue *(Ruta graveolens)*
Sassafras *(Sassafras albidum)*
Senna *(Cassia spp.)*
Willow *(Salix spp.)*
Wisteria *(Wisteria spp.)*

Dahlia 'Taum Sauk' with Monarch

Salvia 'Blue Hill'

Stokesia with Great Spangled Fritillary

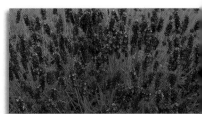

Lavandula angustifolia 'Hidcote'

THE USDA PLANT HARDINESS ZONE MAP OF NORTH AMERICA

Plants are classified according to the amount of cold weather they can handle. For example, a plant listed as hardy to zone 6 will survive a winter in which the temperature drops to minus 10° F.

Warm weather also influences whether a plant will survive in your region. Although this map does not address heat hardiness, in general, if a range of hardiness zones are listed for a plant, the plant will survive winter in the coldest zone as well as tolerate the heat of the warmest zone.

To use this map, find the location of your community, then match the color band marking that area to the zone key at left.

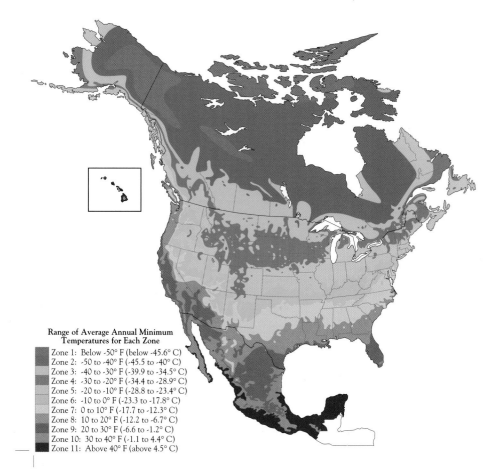

**Range of Average Annual Minimum
Temperatures for Each Zone**

Zone 1: Below -50° F (below -45.6° C)
Zone 2: -50 to -40° F (-45.5 to -40° C)
Zone 3: -40 to -30° F (-39.9 to -34.5° C)
Zone 4: -30 to -20° F (-34.4 to -28.9° C)
Zone 5: -20 to -10° F (-28.8 to -23.4° C)
Zone 6: -10 to 0° F (-23.3 to -17.8° C)
Zone 7: 0 to 10° F (-17.7 to -12.3° C)
Zone 8: 10 to 20° F (-12.2 to -6.7° C)
Zone 9: 20 to 30° F (-6.6 to -1.2° C)
Zone 10: 30 to 40° F (-1.1 to 4.4° C)
Zone 11: Above 40° F (above 4.5° C)

METRIC CONVERSIONS

U.S. Units to Metric Equivalents			Metric Units to U.S. Equivalents		
To Convert From	Multiply By	To Get	To Convert From	Multiply By	To Get
Inches	25.4	Millimeters	Millimeters	0.0394	Inches
Inches	2.54	Centimeters	Centimeters	0.3937	Inches
Feet	30.48	Centimeters	Centimeters	0.0328	Feet
Feet	0.3048	Meters	Meters	3.2808	Feet
Yards	0.9144	Meters	Meters	1.0936	Yards

To convert from degrees Fahrenheit (F) to degrees Celsius (C), first subtract 32, then multiply by ⅝.

To convert from degrees Celsius to degrees Fahrenheit, multiply by ⅘, then add 32.

INDEX

Hummingbird, butterfly, and moth names are boldface. A boldface number indicates a photograph or illustration. An asterisk (*) signifies a main gallery entry.